Creating and thinking critically...

A practical guide to how babies and young children learn

by Di Chilvers

Contents

Published by Practical Pre-School Books, A Division of MA Education Ltd, St Jude's Church, Dulwich Road, Herne Hill, London, SE24 0PB.

Tel: 020 7738 5454

www.practicalpreschoolbooks.com

© MA Education Ltd 2013

Design: Alison Cutler **fonthill**creative 01722 717043

All images © MA Education Ltd. All photos taken by Lucie Carlier with the exception of pages 9, 32, 36, 71 photos taken by Di Chilvers; pages 22-23 photos taken by Anni McTavish.

Page 20: *The Hundred Languages of Children* by Loris Malaguzzi, translated by Lella Gandini, © 1996 Preschools and Infant-toddlers Centers – Istituzione of the Municipality of Reggio Emilia, Italy, published by Reggio Children (www.reggiochildren.it).

All rights reserved. No part of this publication may be reproduced, stored in a retrieval system, or transmitted by any means, electronic, mechanical, photocopied or otherwise, without the prior permission of the publisher.

ISBN 978-1-907241-36-9

Bridgwater College

B0187679

Foreword

Learning and Teaching in the Early Years

Anyone with children's best interests at heart will agree upon the crucial importance of experiences over the earliest years. However, good intentions are not enough to champion young learners. During early childhood, genuinely helpful adult behaviour – 'teaching' – looks very different from the version that suits older children and the classroom environment.

Those adults, who make a real difference, are knowledgeable about child development and committed to a warm relationship with individual children and their families. They are also confident to be led by young children's personal time frames and learning journeys. They pay close attention to the current interests of young girls and boys and their enthusiasm for further discoveries.

The authors of this informative series close the gap of meaning that can exist between familiar phrases and a full understanding of what the words mean in best early years practice. Di Chilvers shows the ways that even the youngest children are already thoughtful and motivated to make sense of their world. Readers are supported to understand how to come alongside babies, toddlers and young children in shared conversation and playful enterprises.

By Jennie Lindon, early years consultant

BRIDGWATER COLLEGE LRC

Introduction

About the series

This book is one of a series of three:

- Playing and exploring

- Active learning

- **Creating and thinking critically**

The starting point for all three books is that babies and young children are already, from birth, creative and competent thinkers and learners – actively involved in their play and gathering information, ideas and knowledge to build their development and learning.

The youngest babies and children are able to use most of the same strategies that will support them as learners all their lives, such as imitating others, playing with things and finding patterns in their experience so they can predict what will happen. These books unpack how children learn and how adults can best support them in being and becoming learners for life.

Playing and exploring, active learning and creating and thinking critically are key characteristics of how children learn and have been linked in recent developmental psychology research to the concept of 'self-regulation'. Self-regulation involves attitudes and dispositions for learning and an ability to be aware of one's own thinking. It also includes managing feelings and behaviour. Self-regulation underpins learning across all areas, developing from birth and supporting lifelong learning (Bronson, 2000).

All babies and young children are different so there is no 'one size fits all' way to foster these characteristics of learning. Young children respond to, and join in with, experiences in different ways depending on a host of factors, including their temperament and the opportunities they have already had. However, the essential message of this book, and the others in the series, is that children (and their families) are entitled to

practitioners who are open to learning from the children with whom they work and who:

- Provide emotional warmth and security

- Tune-in to each unique child by observing and interacting sensitively

- Use observation and knowledge of child development to assess where children are in their learning and plan for next steps and challenges.

All three books provide many illustrative case studies and examples of real-life encounters with children's **active learning**, their **play and exploration** and their **creative and critical thinking**. All these examples show practitioners and children engaged together in supporting and extending children's learning.

Introduction

The characteristics of children's development and learning were embedded in previous English frameworks and recognised in the commitments, which uphold the principles of the EYFS. The Tickell review (2011) of the EYFS drew on recent research and evidence from practitioners and academics across the early years sector in re-emphasising and highlighting those commitments as the **characteristics of effective learning** and they are an important part of the revised EYFS (2012).

As we look at the three characteristics and the underlying aspects of each one, it is important to remember that they are all interlinked. So imagine that the grid below is like a child's piece of weaving, where they have carefully woven individual strands one way and then another so that they are criss-crossing. This is how it should look and is, in reality, how all children develop and learn.

The three characteristics emphasise **how** babies and young children go about the business of learning, rather than simply focusing on **what** they learn.

Practitioners should find these examples useful in reflecting on their own practice and the early years framework with which they work. The books focus particularly on the English Birth to Five framework: the Early Years Foundation Stage (EYFS). However, the characteristics of effective early learning are not tied specifically to any one cultural frame of reference and we hope practitioners working with other frameworks will find the discussion of learning and the ways in which adults support it, transcends national boundaries.

How children develop and learn is about the way in which they grow as thinkers and learners and involves them developing learning dispositions such as: curiosity, persistence, concentration, motivation, confidence and excitement. It is about becoming an independent thinker and learner who is able to make decisions and choices and interpret their ideas and solve problems.

The characteristics of effective learning

Playing and exploring			
Engagement	Finding out and exploring	Playing with what they know	Being willing to 'have a go'
Active learning			
Motivation	Being involved and concentrating	Keeping on trying	Enjoying achieving what they set out to do
Creating and thinking critically			
Thinking	Having their own ideas	Making links	Choosing ways to do things

> "The starting point for all three books is that babies and young children are already, from birth, creative and competent thinkers and learners – actively involved in their play and gathering information, ideas and knowledge to build their development and learning."

If children have all these internal 'tools' at their fingertips as well as a good dose of self-confidence, well-being and resilience then **what** they learn will be encountered in a much more meaningful and enjoyable way.

What children learn is about the actual content or knowledge, so, for example, in the EYFS in England this is the **prime** and **specific** areas of learning – although there are many crossovers, particularly between the content of Personal, Social and Emotional Development and the characteristics. All learning is underpinned by social and emotional development. Generally we can see the **what** of children's learning, or the content, as being like the bricks of a building with the **how** children learn and their social and emotional development as the cement and foundations – without which everything would topple over. The rest of this book explains this in much more depth across the age range from babies to children in school.

Just as the characteristics are woven together, so the three books in this series link together.

For example, in Chapter 1, there is a shared case study about Jago as he plays with a box of balls. Each book looks at Jago's experience and learning from the different perspectives of active learning, playing and exploring and creating and thinking critically.

Throughout all three books there are further case studies, observations, suggestions for supporting children's language development, reflection points and recommended reading.

About this book

Creating and thinking critically looks in depth at what is meant by 'creating and thinking critically', the developmental theory behind this and how it links to good practice.

It unpicks each aspect of creating and thinking critically in terms of what it means and how it can be observed and developed in practice. Some of the key themes in this book are:

- How children's own ideas and interests form the basis of their thinking and learning

- How children play with their ideas and make connections to other aspects of their thinking

- How sustained shared thinking arises out of children's creative interests and how you can support this in practice

- How you can follow children's creative ideas and support their creative and critical thinking.

Chapter 1: What does 'Creating and thinking critically' mean?

"Creativity is rather like play. It anchors us and makes us integrated, whole people. Creativity helps us to get our lives 'together" (Bruce, p.10, 2004).

We begin to see and understand the complexities of children's learning and development when we start to look closely at their creativity and how this plays a central role in their lives from birth. New babies have the rich potential for becoming creative explorers with the curiosity, desire and inclination to

understand the world they are now a part of. But what do we mean by 'creativity' and what does 'thinking critically' look like? We need to know in order to value the creativity of all our children, acknowledge them as competent and capable creators and support their current and future development.

With this in mind, a good starting point is to explore the complex meaning of creativity and critical thinking, the underpinning theory, child development and importantly, how these relate to good practice in early childhood. Chapter 1 focuses on these key aspects:

- The characteristics of children's learning

- The theory behind creativity and thinking critically

- What this looks like in practice as we observe children

- Weaving together the strands of creativity and critical thinking.

The characteristics of children's learning

The characteristics of learning form the backbone of the Early Years Foundation Stage (EYFS) and have been included in the themes and commitments since 2008. They are in the **Learning and Development** theme, which focuses on the following,

'Children develop and learn in different ways and at different rates and all areas of learning and development are equally important and inter-connected'.

There are three commitments that shape the characteristics of children's learning:

- **Play and exploration**

- **Active learning**

- **Creativity and thinking critically.**

It is important to remember that the characteristics do not stand alone, but should be seen as meshing together holistically as children think, develop and learn. As Loris Malaguzzi once explained, when he was referring to children's thinking and learning, it is like a bowl of spaghetti where play, exploration, active learning, creativity and thinking critically all tangle together in one mass. This is how it should be. He went on to say that it is the job of the adult to untangle the spaghetti to understand what they are seeing and what is happening. As we look across the characteristic of creativity and critical thinking in this book, we are 'untangling the spaghetti' in order to make sense of it and improve our knowledge of children and ultimately our practice. It is possible to do this across the other two characteristics in the parallel books: *Active learning* (Helen Moylett) and

> The *how* of children's learning incorporates all the aspects of development which support them in becoming good learners and learning how to learn, including all the skills and dispositions children will need like problem solving, exploring, asking questions and concentrating.

Playing and exploring (Anni McTavish), which, with this title, form the Learning and Teaching in the Early Years series.

Importantly, the characteristics of learning are firmly focused on **how** young children learn and not on **what** they learn. The **how** of children's learning incorporates all the aspects of development which support them in becoming good learners and learning how to learn, including all the skills and dispositions children will need like problem solving, exploring, asking questions and concentrating. For the characteristic of **creating and thinking critically** this also includes children:

- Having their own ideas (Chapter 2)

- Making links (Chapter 3)

- Choosing ways to do things (Chapter 4).

If you imagine children having an internal 'tool kit' for thinking and learning, these are some of the 'tools' they need to help them become motivated, positive and creative learners, tools which they can use confidently at any time, to build their current and future learning and development.

What children learn is bound up in the **seven areas of learning** (EYFS 2012) and mainly consists of all the things they will need to know (knowledge) such as literacy, mathematics and understanding the world. It is much easier for them to learn if they have a full, ready to use 'tool kit' which should also include confidence, self-esteem and well-being.

Chapter 1: What does 'Creating and thinking critically' mean?

As we look more closely at creativity and thinking critically, the **how** of young children's learning will become clearer, showing how essential it is to provide firm foundations for children's development. Indeed the following wise words from Lillian Katz, speaking at a conference in 2011, expressed the critical nature of ensuring children have firm foundations from the beginning, by saying: "Don't start young children on the third floor!". In other words; make sure that the foundations of children's thinking, learning and development are rooted in their early formative years.

Translating theory into practice

When you begin to think about what these words mean in relation to young children, it often helps to spend some time asking yourself the question: "What do I think about my own creativity and critical thinking?". Giving yourself some time to think about the words and their deeper meanings will help you understand their significance for children, especially if you can discuss this with others and listen to their perspectives.

When I consider my own creativity, I think about the ways in which I think, the ideas I have and the avenues I like to explore. I am a creative person but not in the sense that I can draw and paint; rather in the sense that I have ideas I like to express and I can connect up my thinking rather like a jigsaw puzzle. I can reflect on my experiences and talk them through with others, sharing thinking and rising to new challenges. In effect, what I am doing, and have done since I was a child, is to 'hoover' up all kinds of experiences in order to create my own experience. We all do this and we can see it happening very clearly in babies and young children; that is as long as we look.

Malaguzzi (1998), when talking about the early childhood philosophy of Reggio Emila, described creativity as 'a magic spell' which enables children to be expressive, imaginative and full of ideas. Here are a few examples of children's imaginative ideas:

"Why does the sea go in and out?"

"I just got a tube and made it up as I went along. I don't know what it is yet!"

"If you want to remember people you dream about them".

In the world of Reggio Emilia, the practitioners have thought long and hard about the meaning of creativity and creative thinking and for them it includes the following:

- Children who have ideas, thoughts and opinions

- Seeing children's rich potential

- Having a sense of freedom to 'venture beyond the known'

- Imagination – 'friendly exchanges with imagination and fantasy'

- Thinking

- Emotions

- Emerges from 'multiple experiences'

- Expression

- The comparison of ideas and actions with each other

- Negotiating conflict – whose ideas and how do we share them collaboratively?

- Predicting

- Arriving at unexpected solutions.

All of which begin to reveal the complexity of creativity and critical thinking and the richness of children's development and learning, as well as the way in which it interweaves with all their other experiences, like the bowl of spaghetti. Malaguzzi explains it in this way:

> "*Creativity should not be considered a separate mental faculty but a characteristic of our way of thinking, knowing and making choices*" (Edwards, C., Gandini, L., and Forman, G., *The Hundred Languages of Children – The Reggio Emilia Approach – Advanced Reflections*, Ablex Publishing Corporation, p.75, 1998).

Other views of creativity also centre on the development of ideas and how these are supported and developed.

Tina Bruce (2004) refers to children and adults 'hatching ideas' as part of their creative repertoire as they play, explore and talk. Through this we can see how children's creativity is driven from within them, intrinsically, as they make sense of their world. So being creative and thinking critically gives children (and adults) a deep sense of pleasure, satisfaction and achievement, even if it has been a struggle, and the challenge has been demanding.

Jessica's creativity

We can see how Jessica, at 6-months-old, is playing with her ideas about the materials in the treasure basket, puzzling over their properties and 'hoovering' up experiences to add to the ones that she has already and to generate the ones that she will create in the present and the future.

There is an element of Jessica's creativity that is innate, a natural drive within her to be an explorer and discoverer. Indeed we can often see this in its earliest form when babies use every sense, touch, smell, sight, taste and hearing, to find out and then move on to other effective methods of discovery like pointing and asking 'why' questions. In this sense children are like scientists, with the curiosity and courage to experiment, try things out, hypothesise, and problem solve. They are naturally 'programmed' to make meaning of their early experiences, and are very good at it. So we can see that Jessica has the freedom to 'venture beyond the known', is able to express her thinking and will 'arrive at unexpected solutions'. All of which show how competent and capable Jessica is in being and becoming a creative and critical thinker.

The Early Years Foundation Stage (2008) in the themes and principles (4.3 Creativity and critical thinking) describes creativity and critical thinking in the following way:

Pause for thought

Creativity is about having ideas and trying them out, almost like an experiment, to see what happens and how things work.

In order to do this, babies, toddlers and young children need to have many opportunities to play and experiment by themselves and with others.

Links to practice

When you are observing children, including babies and toddlers, can you see the way in which they engage with the experiences around them, experiment with them and put them to good use in their play and explorations?

How do you know children are curious and creative?

What signs/signals can you see?

Chapter 1: What does 'Creating and thinking critically' mean?

When children have opportunities to **play with ideas** in different situations and with a variety of resources, they **discover connections** and come to new and better understandings and **ways of doing things**. Adult support in this process enhances their ability to think critically and ask questions.

This description of creativity emphasises the need for children to play with their ideas, connect them to previous experiences and use them to develop their thinking and understanding. The link is also made between thinking critically and asking questions which is an integral and fundamental part of creativity. The point is made that 'being creative' involves the whole curriculum and not just the activities children undertake in the 'creative area' like painting, collage and box modelling. So if we unpick these terms even further we end up with the following aspects of creativity, thinking critically and being creative.

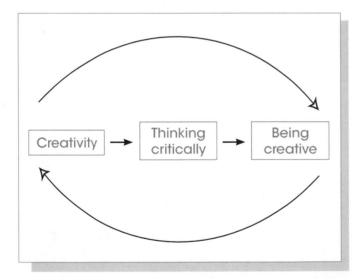

Creativity can be viewed as being part of a child's personality, their character, temperament and make-up and because of this inherent trait, creativity is bound up in the development of self-identity and self-esteem. In psychology, creativity is described as finding a sense of purpose and direction in life (Miell et al., 2002) which every person has to develop for themselves and leads to a human desire for self-fulfilment, in effect *'to become everything one is capable of becoming'* (p.203). So it is linked to seeing the child as having rich potential with many possibilities for their own 'ideas, thoughts and opinions'. Being creative gives children a sense of purpose and direction, which they need to hold onto to enable them to become positive, happy and effective thinkers and learners.

curiosity excitement
perseverance
self-motivation
playfulness
confidence
interests
happiness
independence
eagerness
resilience
calmness
problem solving
reasoning
attentiveness
excitement
cooperativeness
exploration
challenging
thoughtfulness
sociable imaginative
communicative
involvement
being expressive autonomous

Children's dispositions

The innate qualities that children have, become their dispositions and attitudes for learning and life and are fundamental to being a creative and critical thinker. Dispositions will contribute to the child's sense of who they are and what they can be and as such are bound up with their developing self-identity and self-belief that they are competent and capable thinkers and learners. The box above gives some examples of dispositions.

Dispositions can be explained as the ways in which children *'become interested, excited and motivated by their learning'*

(EYFS, 2008, PSED Learning and Development card) which we can see when children stick at a challenging activity and then let out a shriek of delight when they have completed it. Frequently, as we observe children we can see these dispositions in the ways that they are curious, involved and thoughtful, just like Jessica and Jago later in this chapter.

In more complex terms, dispositions are *'habits of the mind or tendencies to respond to situations in characteristic ways'* (Katz and Chard, 1989). If we unpick this definition, it means that children have behavioural characteristics and attitudes which come from within them (they are intrinsic) and which we can often see as we observe them. So, for example, if we were looking for a creative disposition (behaviours), given the right opportunities, children would be curious and interested in the world around them. As a result, they will be motivated and confident to explore their immediate world and the people and things within it. They would be inquisitive, imaginative and playful, seeking out new ideas and ways of doing things.

Dispositions are acquired and developed as children 'wallow' in the experiences around them and from the people who care for and nurture them. They are so important to children as they determine how they develop as a person and as a learner; they shape the child's motivation to learning. Clearly we would want all children to be immersed in experiences and environments which nurture these positive dispositions and support children's development to become the competent and capable thinkers and learners that we know they can be. We would want their 'tool kits' to be full of positive dispositions but this may not always be the case.

Dispositions are an important way of seeing and understanding children's learning and development, as they tell us a great deal more about the depth of their thinking and understanding, far more than looking at superficial outcomes like counting to five or knowing the names of colours.

Dispositions weave aspects of children's development together (it's the spaghetti model again!) so that we can see many things in one disposition. For example all children have the creative disposition of 'curiosity', which covers a whole range of possibilities in terms of their learning. Having a 'curious disposition' means that you will be a keen explorer of materials, activities and people. This will then influence relationships with other children and social awareness and behaviour; children may then become more confident and outgoing, resulting in raised self-esteem and positive well-being. As we can see the

knock-on effects or 'ripples' make important connections to other aspects of development. It's not a neat and tidy process but then development and learning isn't and nor should it be.

Creativity as a process

There are many views of creativity as a 'process'. A helpful way of thinking about creativity as a process is to imagine it as a journey where you have to navigate from one place to another but there are no shortcuts. The vision I have in my head is that this process is more about slowly, navigating the beautiful, meandering lanes of the country side rather than hurtling up the motorway as fast as you can, arriving at your destination without even remembering the journey.

The process (the doing) of creativity is far more relevant and important to children than the end product (the outcome), as this is where they will be involved in thinking critically, developing their understanding and learning. For them, the outcome at the end is just the 'cherry on the cake', it is the actual 'creative doing' that is the cake or the main part of the process.

For example, I recently observed two children playing imaginatively in the home corner; Ruth was the cat and Maya the mummy. They were deeply involved in creating their play and deciding what the cat would eat and where it would sleep. I listened and watched, taking photographs of their play and

writing down the conversation between the two. When the play had finished I went to talk to Ruth and Maya to say how much I had enjoyed watching them play and the kind way that the mummy had looked after the cat. I was keen to share the photographs with them and asked them if they would like to see them. They both stopped what they were doing (now at the computer) and said "no thanks"! The creative moment had passed for them and they were now on to the next thing – having stored up their imaginative ideas and conversations to be repeated and developed another day. The process of the play that they had created was the 'cake' and they were not that bothered about the 'outcomes' I was offering to show them.

Duffy (1998) outlines a model of the creative process, which includes the dispositions of curiosity and exploration and has four levels. Models like this can help to explain the complexities and layers of children's development and learning: 'start from the bottom and work upwards' (see diagram).

Children's imagination

Being imaginative is also a disposition and has a significant part to play in creativity and thinking critically. Children are naturally imaginative and very able to engage in imaginative play at an early age, as we can see from the way in which these 23-30-month-old children in a Reggio Emilia toddler centre played with the trees. They were involved in a project called 'Surprise in the City' and were looking at the trees in the park. The trees were then 'brought back' to the setting by projecting a film of them on to the white walls of the room, the children played in the trees and 'sat with them to keep them company'.

Creativity

What can I create or invent? Children at this point are making new connections and joining up their thinking. They are discovering new ways and approaches to solving problems and deepening their understanding. This is where children are fully engaged in thinking critically and following their interests.

Play

What can I do with this? Children immerse themselves in their play and try out their ideas, test their hypotheses and make adjustments. This will be initiated by the child, can be spontaneous and may look as though there is no real focus or plan. This is the process in action and no end product or outcome is necessary it is an opportunity to practice, repeat and consolidate their thinking, skills and knowledge.

Exploration

Finding out? Gathering information using all their senses, investigating objects, events or ideas. Watching others can also be part of the investigation.

Curiosity

What is it? Children's attention is focused and they have an interest in something or someone – they want to know more.

Start Here

Pause for thought

Observation is the key way in which we can find out about children's creativity and the creative process (on the right) helps us to see this happening. We can see the process in Jessica's play with the treasure basket and Jago's play with the balls (see the case study at the end of the chapter). Have a look at the sequence of pictures and see if you can identify the creative process described above. How can you tell she/he is curious and her attention is focused? What can you see that indicates she/he is exploring and finding out?

Links to practice

In your everyday observations, see if you can see this process happening (or at least parts of it) as you watch the child/children.

They then decided to trace/draw the trees on the wall so that they wouldn't disappear when the lights were turned on. The children's imaginative ideas surprised the adults who were not expecting them to want to re create the trees or stop them from disappearing. The children's ideas and voices illustrate their imagination very well:

Sara (2yrs, 2mths): *"This is a very big cherry tree. It has long branches which go up, up, up really high".*

Alessia (2yrs, 6mths): *"Look at my tree. My tree is in the shape of a cherry".*

Giovanni (2yrs, 5mths): *"Look at my tree. My tree is in the shape of a tree".*

Children's imagination and imaginative play are one of the most important tools for creativity. Using their imagination enables children to put into action their ideas and make them visible for everyone to see. The connections they make in their imaginative play help them to visualise and construct their thinking, make sense of their world, and create narratives and stories that we can see, just like the cat and the mummy that Ruth and Maya created.

Claxton (2000) suggests that children have an 'internal imagination' which combines their thinking and ideas and enables them to think things through. This is quite a sophisticated thing to do but which we can observe happening in children's play. He goes on to say, that *'learning by imagination is the ability to extend what we know, and can do, by creating imaginary worlds'*.

There are many other dispositions that support the development of creativity apart from having ideas, being curious and being imaginative. Again if you go back to thinking about your own creativity, consider the dispositions you have that support the creative you; interestingly not all dispositions are positive. I wonder how many practitioners will consider themselves to have little creativity – as they

focus on a narrower view of being creative and dismiss their capabilities just because they can't draw! I hope it is clear that we are viewing creativity in its wider form which has many more facets that are inherent in all of us, even if you have to look harder – it will be there.

The following table highlights some more dispositional characteristics and what they might look like in practice when you are observing children.

Thinking critically

Creativity and being creative always involves thinking critically. One way to look at this is that **creativity** and all its dispositional elements, along with being creative (yet to be discussed) are all in the 'pot'. **Thinking critically** gives it a good stir and enables children (and adults) to transform their understanding, solve problems and come up with new ideas and solutions. Through this 'stirring' we are creating, understanding and deepening our thinking, learning and development. We are undertaking a 'cognitive act' or a 'meta-cognitive process' which means we are 'thinking about thinking' (Robson, p.82, 2006). It is how children come to be aware of themselves as thinkers, along with being able to describe their thinking, ideas and fascinations and to make them visible in some way. We can see Jessica and Jago thinking critically as

Chapter 1: What does 'Creating and thinking critically' mean?

Dispositions that support the development of creativity and critical thinking

Disposition	Dispositional characteristic	What this might look like
Being an explorer	Exploration is an in-built drive for babies, toddlers and young children – they were born to explore. This is one of the main ways that they find out about how things work, who people are and what they can do.	As you watch children (babies and toddlers) you will notice that they: ● Are curious, like to look, watch and listen. ● Will frequently put things in their mouths, using the sensitive feelings they have in their lips and tongue to find out about objects and materials. ● Will use all their senses to find out and make sense of the world around them. ● Can make sense of their immediate world and the people, places and things within it.
Being an experimenter	Children, babies and toddlers are natural experimenters with very similar skills as scientists. They experiment through trying their ideas out, wondering what will happen and asking questions like why? And what if? They are not afraid to try things out and 'test' their hypotheses, then look for solutions. They are full of wonder and open to possibilities with endless curiosity.	As you watch children (babies and toddlers) you will notice that they are: ● Always looking and soaking up what is happening around them. ● Trying things out through their play and will often repeat their actions. ● Fascinated and absorbed by things we may not see as adults, for example they may always want to roll or throw objects because they want to find out what happens.
Being an inventor	Every child is unique, with their own personality, ideas and perspectives and because of this they are natural inventors. Being an explorer and experimenter also means that you are an inventor. Children create their ideas from the way they see the world – they recreate the things they have seen and heard and the people they meet putting their own 'spin' on their creativity. The world according to them which is unique and inventive.	As you watch children (babies and toddlers) you will notice that they are: ● Puzzling out the ways in which to do things, how to balance a brick, how to make the bike move, how to get what they want. ● Always trying to do things and will keep coming back to previous attempts and experiences. ● Sometimes cross and frustrated because things go wrong or they don't work or another child gets in the way. ● Often surprising you with what they say, make and create.

Chapter 1: What does 'Creating and thinking critically' mean?

Dispositions that support the development of creativity and critical thinking...

Disposition	Dispositional characteristic	What this might look like
Being independent	Children are independent in that they have unique and original ideas and ways of doing things. They have a sense of 'agency' as they get to know themselves, what they can do, having the confidence and self esteem to reach their potential.	As you watch children (babies and toddlers) you will notice that they are: • Fascinated and interested in things which are unique to them, for example they may have schematic interests which are focused on hiding, covering themselves and others up and enveloping objects. • Motivated to explore their own interests through child initiated play and activities, for example having an interest in dinosaurs. • Happy to be by themselves but are able to play and collaborate with others. • Gaining deep satisfaction and pleasure from being involved.
Being persistent	When children, including babies and toddlers, become very involved and absorbed in what they are doing they stick at it and persist even when it is a challenge. This means that they are able to continue to develop their creative ideas – their ideas flow and actions are often repeated.	As you watch children (babies and toddlers) you will notice that they are: • Not easily distracted, their attention is focused on what they are doing or who they are talking to, they may look away but will then return to the matter in hand. • Concentrating for long periods. • Still involved in the activity even if it is difficult or there are challenges such as a tower falling over all the time. • Able to 'go with the flow', where one idea leads to another.
Being resourceful	Above all, children are resourceful, finding new ways to do things and work things out. This is a crucial part of creativity. Children need to be able to take measured risks and make mistakes otherwise they will not move forward. Making a mistake and having another go are very effective ways of learning maybe more so than getting things right all the time. This all means that children are flexible in the way they do things and open to change – this is what moves thinking forward.	As you watch children (babies and toddlers) you will notice that they are: • Trying out different ways to make things work or get what they want. • Persistent, sticking at something until they are happy with it. • Able to ask for help or support from other children and adults. • Still confident to have a 'go' even if it went wrong the first time. • Able to remember what went wrong and use this in other situations. • Not afraid to try.

Chapter 1: What does 'Creating and thinking critically' mean?

Dispositions which support the development of creativity and critical thinking...

Disposition	Dispositional characteristic	What this might look like
Being energetic	Children are energetic and not just physically! Their brains are always on the go as their creativity and ideas find ways to express themselves. They have energy for life, learning and growing. Their creativity is energetic because of all the things we have considered here and many more.	As you watch children (babies and toddlers) you will notice that they are: • Energetic, enthusiastic and excited. • Motivated from within and having an innate drive to discover. • Keen to persist at what interests them and are not always happy to stop. • Eager to repeat and come back to activities, places and people. • Usually exhausted after energetic periods of activity and can be tearful, grumpy or very excited.
Being a communicator	Children are communicating all the time (including babies and toddlers). They want to communicate their ideas and actions and can do this through their play, talking to themselves and with others, through their conversations, through their creations. Indeed they are competent and capable communicators from the beginning using their 'One Hundred Languages' (Loris Malaguzzi). Talking and other forms of communication generate more ideas and confirm the ones that they have. In fact, creativity is about communicating your unique ideas.	As you watch children (babies and toddlers) you will notice that they are: • Expressing themselves, their thoughts and ideas. • Making their ideas visible through talk, play, movement, bricks and blocks, paint and clay etc. • Very keen to communicate in some way to you, for example through their facial expressions, body language, babbling, talking. • Involved in play and using this to express themselves, their feelings, emotions, ideas etc. • Talking with other children and adults and reflecting on what they have done or what has happened and coming up with new ideas or ways of doing things together.

they explore the materials in curious and imaginative ways and then come to new ways of thinking about them.

Creative thinkers will relish a challenge, and for babies and toddlers these may be small challenges (small from the adult's perspective but not small for them) like reaching out for a toy or trying to put the lid on a box. They are not afraid to have a go and take a risk or make a mistake. They also have belief in themselves and are confident and capable builders of their own ideas; with the ability to deal with uncertainty (Will my tower fall if I add another brick? Am I strong enough to carry two full buckets?) and ultimately they succeed in having full 'mastery' (understanding) of what they are doing and thinking.

'Creative people….are good problem solvers. They like adventures with new ideas…and are fascinated by the creative experience of thinking of new ideas' (Bruce, p.15, 2004).

Thinking critically is also a process of construction! The early years philosophy of Reggio Emilia views the child as an 'active constructor of knowledge' who is very capable of interpreting their own world, their own ideas, their own thinking. Children do this through a process of co-construction, which means building your thinking together, with others; children or adults. Malaguzzi (p.68, 1998) described this process as being like a game of table tennis.

Building creative thinking together

Imagine that you are playing with a child in your setting, let's call her 'Emily', and she is four-years-old. You see that she is interested in the frost on the grass in the garden. She bends down to look at it and says: "the grass is shining"; this is the first 'hit of the ball'. She is batting it to you and showing that she is interested in what has happened to the grass. Now you have to 'catch the ball': listen to what Emily is saying and also take an interest. You might say: "oh yes it is, I wonder why that happened?"– now you are 'batting the ball' back to Emily. Emily sees that you are interested and 'bats her ball' back to you: "the grass got painted in the night when I was asleep". Now it's your turn: "I think it might have been but I wonder who painted it?". You are returning the idea that Emily has proposed. It is important not to dismiss her ideas and suggestions, but to accept them and take them on a bit further to extend her thinking; this is where you are building (constructing) the thinking together. Emily may look a bit puzzled at your response but this is okay as it means that she has to think hard for a reason as to who, or what, may have painted the grass in the night. She may respond by saying: "I don't know but it's very cold and wet".

The conversation and thinking will progress as you 'bat' a response back to Emily and she then 'bats' it back to you. The important thing is to make sure that you don't 'drop the ball' which means that you need to show your interest and become involved, not by telling Emily the answer, but by trying to get her to think about the possibilities and hypotheses as to why the grass looks as though it has been painted. Ultimately you may 'bat the ball' by reading her a story about the frost or getting Emily to take photographs and take them home to ask her mum.

> **Creative thinkers will relish a challenge, and for babies and toddlers these may be small challenges like reaching out for a toy or trying to put the lid on a box. They are not afraid to have a go and take a risk or make a mistake.**

You can see the thinking being constructed in this example, with the ball being 'batted and returned' as Emily thinks critically about her (and your) ideas and suggestions. These occasions, usually started by a child's or children's interest in something, lead to episodes of **sustained shared thinking** (Siraj-Blatchford, 2002, 2003, 2009), **joint problem solving** (Wood and Attfield, 2005) or **possibility thinking** (Craft, 2006). These terms, which can sound complex, are actually very helpful and describe the table tennis process very well; ultimately it is about sharing thinking and the possibilities

Chapter 1: What does 'Creating and thinking critically' mean?

which arise from that, as well as it being a problem solving process. Craft's (p.13, 2010) possibility thinking is about children finding and solving problems with each other and adults then asking 'possibility questions' to deepen thinking. This is a creative process that involves the imagination and thinking skills and leads to thinking critically.

Setting problems and solving them are an integral part of thinking critically along with the ability to reason things through and find out why things happen, how they work and what else you can do with them. As we can see with Emily's possibility thinking, she has set a problem; the frost on the grass, then sets about solving it with the adult's support and is heavily involved in reasoning out what has happened and what may have caused it. Being able to reason is an important skill, which begins at a young age. For example, we can see babies puzzling out where the doll went as it fell behind the sofa and then realising that they can find it, it's just hidden. They then need plenty of opportunities in play to practise and refine their reasoning skills so that it can be used in increasingly more complex ways.

To solve a problem, and set one, children need to be able to think critically and creatively. The most natural and motivating way to do this is through their play. If you observe children during their play, their problem setting, problem solving and reasoning skills will be there; you just need to look for them.

Take a look back at Jessica as she tries to find out about the objects in her basket; she is very focused and highly involved in finding out what the materials can do. You can almost 'see' her thinking as she puzzles over the black reel and looks inside the small red bag. Jessica is a problem-setter and problem-solver and now, aged three, has moved on to even greater problems to solve like 'how do I tell Uncle David to be quiet when I am trying to think?'. This is just part of her everyday life – solving the problems that come along as she plays.

In effect, what is happening as children reason and solve problems is that they learn something new and connect it to all their other previous experiences to use again another day. And if they keep doing this their critical thinking will become sophisticated and finely tuned. This is a fundamental part of creativity and being able to think critically.

We know that young children's imagination has a substantial part to play across all three aspects of creativity, being creative and thinking critically, but it is particularly crucial in supporting the development of abstract thinking. Abstract thinking is a sophisticated and complex development for young children, as they move from the concrete, object-led world of their

Pause for thought

Imaginative play is one of the main ways in which children's creativity and critical thinking is put into action. It is the way that they make sense of the world around them, particularly in moving from concrete experiences in the here and now to more abstract experiences, which involve symbols including letters and numbers.

Links to practice

In your setting do you provide rich opportunities for imaginative play for babies, toddlers and young children?

Are there plenty of open-ended materials so that they can create dens, space ships and castles as well as materials that transform them into the monster, hero or wizard?

early years to an increasingly more abstract one that is full of symbols which carry meaning, like words and numbers. Vygotsky (1978) explains it this way:

'The projection into an imaginary world stretches their conceptual abilities and involves a development in their abstract thought. The complexity involved in this process makes imagination the highest level of early development' (Duffy, p.53, 1998).

Children's imaginative play is a wonderful mechanism for helping them to think creatively about some very challenging abstract concepts that they will come across all too soon, like letters, sounds/phonics, writing and mathematical processes such as addition and subtraction. What happens in their imaginative play is that children begin to use all kinds of objects around them to substitute for something else – so the chairs become a train, the box becomes a castle and the mud becomes a magic potion. It is this shift in children's thinking that helps them recognise and understand the challenge of accepting that when we write 'cat' we mean the furry thing with four legs that goes 'meow'. The child reasons that, if I can be flexible enough in my thinking to accept that I can use an object to represent something I want it to be, then I can accept that these squiggles and marks can have meaning. It is indeed a sophisticated level of thinking critically and one that all children need to master and feel confident about doing as it will become a massive part of their lives. As adults we have long forgotten the cognitive struggle we had in our early years to understand the squiggles and sounds of letters and then put them together as we read stories or wrote a sentence.

As the child's brain makes this leap from the 'here and now' to the more abstract, it also allows them to think in different ways and from different perspectives. Having other perspectives gives children a valuable tool to see their world in different ways, understand the views of others and think more flexibly, which supports their creative and critical thinking. It also helps them to be collaborative so that, as they play, explore and interact, they are doing their problem solving and thinking together which is far more effective than doing it on your own!

It has been suggested that the 'two most important processes in critical thinking' are:

1. learning how to question, when to question, and what questions to ask

2. learning how to reason, when to use reasoning, and what reasoning methods to use.

(Fisher. p.173, 1990 in Robson, 2006.)

Children, when they are very young, are good at asking questions – often starting before they can talk by using their pointing finger to direct their curiosity. They then progress on to the wonderful 'why' question as their thinking and language become more developed. The creative questions they ask are crucial to thinking critically and pursuing answers or solutions to the problems they want to solve, but they have to be the children's questions in order for them to develop as critical thinkers. As soon as adults start dominating the question-asking, the children lose a sense of themselves as competent and capable question askers; they quickly learn to become question-answerers. This is a truly significant loss to them as creative and critical thinkers.

Children's questions allow them opportunities to express their ideas and think out loud and contribute to the development of their reasoning skills. As they bounce ideas and questions to each other, and to adults, their ability to reason develops and becomes more complex, as we saw in the example of sustained shared thinking with Emily and the frost. Reasoning through collaborative discussion is a central part of the early years philosophy in Reggio Emilia. Children

Chapter 1: What does 'Creating and thinking critically' mean?

The Hundred Languages of Children

The child
is made of one hundred.
The child has
a hundred languages
a hundred hands
a hundred thoughts
a hundred ways of thinking
of playing, of speaking.
A hundred always a hundred
ways of listening
of marvelling of loving
a hundred joys
for singing and understanding
a hundred worlds
to discover
a hundred worlds
to invent a hundred worlds
to dream
but they steal ninety-nine.
The schools and the culture
separate the head from the body.
They tell the child:
to think without hands
to do without head
to listen and not to speak
to understand without joy
to love and to marvel
only at Easter and Christmas.

Loris Malaguzzi (1920-1994)

Reggio Emilia – Northern Italy

(translated by Lella Gandini)

will spend long periods of time talking together (it is called a dialogue) as they bounce their ideas around and develop their thinking, as we can see from the following example of Domenico, Benedetta and Elisa (all aged 5) explaining their drawings of a crowd of people:

Domenico: Oh no!

Elisa (anticipating the others' criticism): Mine's just a LITTLE crowd.

Benedetta: But you made the people all going the same way!

Elisa: They're all friends, so they're all going the same way!

Benedetta: But in a crowd, the people aren't all friends or relatives, you know.

(Spaggiari and Rinaldi, C., p.144, 1996.)

Being creative

This third aspect: 'Being creative', is the one which most early years practitioners will be familiar with, will have focused on with children and is related to the area of learning in the EYFS (2008 and 2012). It is part of the everyday view of children's creativity which supports children's artistic pursuits like painting, drawing, box modelling, collage and music which, as we have seen in this chapter, is not an accurate or full understanding of children's creativity. Of course this is a crucial part of children's learning and development and one that brings them, their parents and practitioners a great deal of joy and creative expression but it is only a part of the complex 'jigsaw' of creating and thinking critically.

It is through the 'arts' that we express many of our inner thoughts, ideas and feelings and for young children this is one of the key ways in which they make themselves 'heard'. *The Hundred Languages of Children*, opposite, expresses this.

Malaguzzi gives us a real sense of the rich potential of children's creativeness and their eager motivation to try new things and express their ideas in so many unique and inspired ways, but as the poem goes on he says much of this is 'stolen' (see opposite).

Interestingly, the area of creative development in the EYFS (2008) has now been renamed 'Expressive arts and design'

(EYFS 2012) which seems to reinforce the view that children's creativeness is mainly about song, music, dance, colour, texture, design, shape and form. However, there is a reinstated focus on 'Being imaginative', which supports and encourages children to 'represent their own ideas, thoughts and feelings through design and technology, art, music, dance, role play and stories' (p.9, 2012). This is an important inclusion as we have already seen how children's imagination plays a significant part in their ability to think critically and understand the abstract world they live in.

It is important that we see children's creativity in a much broader way than just through one of the areas of learning. As we have seen in this chapter the nature of creativity and thinking critically has many layers and is quite complex so 'being creative' is just one part of a much bigger picture. The case study of Jago attending his developmental movement session (page 22) helps us to see this. As you read through the case study think about the aspects of creativity:

- creativity;

- thinking critically;

- being creative;

and how they are brought together through his play.

Pause for thought

The Hundred Languages of Children was written by Loris Malaguzzi to express the view that all children, from the moment they are born, are competent and capable participants in their own thinking, learning and development.

Links to practice

As you read the *Hundred Languages* think about the following:

What do you think Malaguzzi means by 'hundred languages'?

Talk this through with your colleagues and think about the 'languages' that you enable children to use in your setting.

If 'ninety-nine' are stolen – what do you think children are left with and how will this affect their creativity and critical thinking?

Communication and language

It is impossible to consider children's creativity and critical thinking without making the connection with the development of their communication and language. Language and thinking are partners as they collectively support the development of each other – talk is a key way in which babies, toddlers and young children make their thoughts and feelings visible and thinking helps to clarify, develop and extend talk. It is a two-way process. For example, as toddlers develop their talk they may call everything with four legs a dog (even when it's a cat) but gradually, through their thinking and developing understanding of what a dog is, they realise that a cat is something completely different and is called a cat. They have come to know the 'dogness' of dog and the 'catness of cat', which is part of developing their critical thinking as well as their language.

Creating and thinking critically require children to understand the world around them and make sense of the many things they come into contact with. In the same way, they also have to make sense of talking and what sounds and words mean as we say them; then attach those words to actual things – like dogs and cats. As adults we understand words (well most of them) and their meanings but children have to acquire this, and do so in an amazingly short space of time. Interestingly, children will use the same strategies and thinking for learning language as they begin to learn to read and write. What this means is that the roots of children's literacy begin in 'the richness of early non-verbal communication and the power of children's thinking and feeling in infancy' (Whitehead, M. in Moyles, J., p.270, 2007).

The following are just some of the complex components of language and communication:

Conversational language – where children's talk is informal and part of their everyday experiences with one or more people it actually involves rich opportunities for thinking.

Formulating ideas – talking generates ideas and thinking at any age. A baby babbles with delight as she controls a game

CASE STUDY – The strands of creating and thinking critically in practice

In the following case study you will see the practitioner's observation of Jago using photographs and written notes. The written observational notes with the links to creating and thinking critically are in the boxes. These notes show how we need to look at what Jago may be thinking about, his interests and fascinations and his development.

Jago (12mths) is at a baby movement session with his mum. At the end of the session, most people have left. Jago and his mum Natalie are getting ready to go, when he notices the cardboard box full of balls and watches a practitioner put a ball in the box.

What he does next illustrates his creative and critical thinking and shows many of the aspects discussed in this chapter.

Pause for thought

As you think about the observation of Jago, have a look back at this chapter to see if you can identify some of the characteristics of his creativity and critical thinking. Are you surprised by the depth and detail of his thinking? Can you see this happening when you observe the children in your setting?

Jago's face lights up and he crawls swiftly over to the box. He uses his right and then his left hand to touch the red ball, which is soft and light.

Jago is curious about the balls and wants to find out more – we can see this by the way he is stretching out to touch them and the interested expression on his face. He is exploring the ball through his sense of touch and sight and will use this as an opportunity to be a 'scientist', experimenting with the ball to see what it can do and adding this to his other knowledge of what balls do.

Jago touches and moves the ball with both hands pulling the ball towards him, with a look of real concentration on his face, and manages to roll it over the edge.

We can see Jago's desire and inclination to make sense of his world and 'hoover' up new pieces of information to add to his existing ideas.

He is now constructing his own thinking by showing his interest in the ball and playing with it.

The ball rolls away from him across the floor, he immediately turns and crawls quickly after it.

As Jago plays, the ball rolls away and a new action is required. He sees that the ball rolls, adds this to his thinking and then 'hatches' his own idea to follow it. He is actively solving the problem of the rolling ball by following it and shows us how competent he is in constructing his own thinking and learning. He is thinking critically.

He brings the red ball back, crawling, pushing and pinching it between his fingers to move it as he crawls. Then Jago puts the ball back into the box – this takes quite a lot of effort.

He then lifts out one of silver balls, which is solid and shiny; then another, both balls are then side by side in front of him. He looks very pleased and Natalie, his mother, shares his delight by smiling, she does not rush him, and waits for him to put the balls back into the box again one at a time.

Jago now makes an important connection in his thinking by checking out the silver balls. He has some ideas or hypotheses about the red ball and now wants to apply them to the silver ones. He plays with the possibilities (possibility thinking) and is happy and very satisfied with his findings. He has shown many dispositions in his encounter with the balls including curiosity, involvement, persistence, pleasure and happiness.

Jago's mum was supportive and patient as she waited for him to make his careful exploration of the balls.

Links to practice

What do you think Jago is interested in and what are the possibilities for the next session? How would you support his creativity and thinking? This would be a good activity to undertake with other practitioners, so that you can share your own thinking and ideas.

Chapter 1: What does 'Creating and thinking critically' mean?

> **Communication isn't just about talking; it includes the many ways in which children make their needs, feelings and ideas known (non-verbal communication).**

Communication isn't just about talking; it includes the many ways in which children make their needs, feelings and ideas known (non-verbal communication). For babies, the communicative act of crying is their language of choice, with a sophisticated range of cries containing different meanings, 'I am hungry' or 'I am tired' or 'I am bored and I want to play'. As children grow and develop they use play as one of their main avenues of communication where we gain an insight into thought processes and thinking. As we observe children, there are many signs and signals communicated through facial expression and body language, as well as feelings and emotions. We often know that a child is frustrated with something long before they can actually tell us, just by watching for the signs.

The links between creating and thinking critically and communication and language will be made throughout the book but it is helpful to think of the two as inextricably connected:

Children who are helped to be skilful communicators are able to find their voice and to make meaning. Competent learners are able to make connections, be imaginative and creative and to represent their experiences, feelings and relationships (Bruce, p.9, 2004).

This chapter has covered some of the theoretical elements, which underpin the development of creativity and critical thinking in young children. It is essential that we have a good

of 'I drop the rattle and you pick it up' and a four-year-old will chatter as he tries to work out how to make the wheels turn on the car he has just made.

Confirming and clarifying what we think – Conversations with others help to confirm and clarify what we think. By speaking about experiences, including learning, young children can reaffirm themselves and gain confidence in what they are doing. They can check and re-check their ideas collaboratively.

Reflection – Speaking involves reflection; thinking about past experiences or what they have just done and engaging in conversation: "I remember when…" or "When I was a baby did I…", "The last time I did this it…".

Making ideas and thinking visible – In a conversation the child's ideas and thinking are made visible and are usually related to something which is of interest to them and based in the reality and context of their lives. For example: "Why does the snow disappear?" or "why can't I jump as high as the cat?". It is only by giving children endless opportunities to talk that we can begin to understand what is going on in their heads.

Building confidence and self-esteem – Confidence and self-esteem arise out of being listened to and accepted. One of the key ways in which this happens is through children's conversation. If children's own conversations are accepted they quickly learn that their views, ideas and talk are valued. Through conversation children gain affirmation and the courage to contribute as well as being able to express their own needs, wishes and thoughts. They will become more in touch with themselves and develop a sense of positive well-being (Adapted from Chilvers, D., 2006).

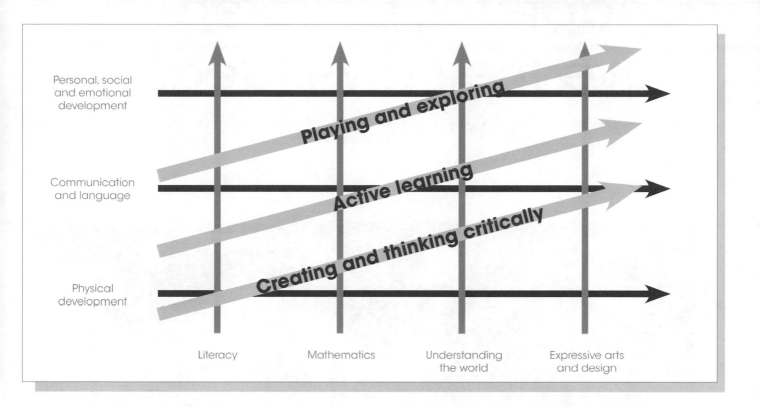

understanding of the developmental theory behind children's thinking and learning so that we can understand them better, tune-in to where they are and support their next steps.

We also need to know how all the pieces fit together as we work within the Early Years Foundation Stage (EYFS) with the three characteristics of effective learning and teaching:

● Playing and exploring;

● Active learning;

● Creating and thinking critically;

and the seven areas of learning:

● Personal, social and emotional development

● Physical development

● Communication and language

● Literacy

● Mathematics

● Understanding the world

● Expressive arts and design.

The young children we work with don't actually need to know these details; the structure of the EYFS is there to ensure that what we offer children, in whatever setting, is of the highest quality and appropriate to support children's thinking and learning.

What is important is that we 'weave' together all these aspects so that they are viewed in the same way as children's learning – holistically. Remember the bowl of spaghetti – this metaphor also applies to the way in which we interpret the EYFS and the areas of learning. All of these components should come together in a seamless philosophy, which views children's learning and development as interwoven. In reality it should look like the above diagram.

The following chapters will look in detail at the three aspects of creating and thinking critically:

● Children have their own ideas

● Children make links

● Children choosing ways to do things.

Chapter 2: Children have their own ideas

Young children, including babies and toddlers, are bursting with ideas and an intrinsic need to find out, explore and understand the world around them. We can see this clearly in their facial expressions, their physical movements, the way they use all their senses and their efforts to communicate so they can 'test' out their ideas and thoughts in order to understand, develop and learn. In this way, all children, from the moment they are born, are competent, creative and motivated to be creative and critical thinkers.

This chapter will look in much more depth at the following questions:

- What does 'children having their own ideas' actually mean?

- How can we see this as we observe babies, toddlers and young children and what does this tell us about children's creativity and critical thinking?

- How can adults (practitioners, teachers, parents) support, develop and extend children's ideas?

- How does the enabling environment support, develop and extend children's ideas?

Children having their own ideas

One of the key aspects of being creative and thinking critically is the generation of ideas and thinking about your ideas. Ideas come from within the child and are 'born' from their curiosity, imagination, exploration and interest in the people, places and things around them. As such, they are a real window into the mind of the child and what they are thinking. Children's ideas tell us a great deal about their thinking, development and learning; which is why we need to pay attention to their ideas, observe them as they unfold and use them as key starting points for development and learning. Froebel (1782-1852) a German educationalist who developed the concept of kindergartens, believed strongly that children's ideas were represented and made real through their imaginative and creative play. He said that through being creative and imaginative 'we give body…to thought…we render visible the invisible' (Duffy, p.21, 1998).

Children's ideas may not be new in the sense that no-one else has ever thought of them, but they are original and unique for that child at that time. Every child is unique and will have their own experiences and interpretations of what they are thinking and their responses to the people, places and things they come into contact with. The significant thing is that we recognise children's unique ideas, value them and follow them through.

Natalia's flow of ideas illustrates well the power of creativity and creative thinking and what can happen when we tune into children's ideas and follow them. Csikszentmihalyi (1996) has written at length about the 'state of flow' in humans ability to become so engrossed in what they are doing that they become unaware of time or distractions and are fully focused on the task in hand. This is the same for children, where they become deeply involved in something, usually that they have initiated, and they become lost in it, concentrating for long periods and persisting even when the going gets tough.

Ferre Laevers (1994) has focused on children's involvement and engagement in their play and activities and created the involvement scales which characterise the flow of a child's thinking through observing how intrinsically motivated they are, how they concentrate and persist at what they are doing and how fascinated and absorbed they are in the activity. We can see many of these characteristics in Natalia as she follows her ideas and connects them together.

When we take note of, and respond to, children's ideas, including babies and toddlers, we have tapped into one of the best sources of creativity and creative thinking, far more inspiring and meaningful to children than if we had spent hours planning detailed, overly-structured activities for a six-week period. Craft's research on enabling possibility thinking with four-year-olds has shown this to be true as children 'were seen to be generating ideas, leading on possibilities, and maintaining interest, focus, ownership in the evolution of ideas' (p.54, 2012).

Describing children's ideas

There are many different ways of describing children's ideas, that respect and value the complexity and uniqueness of children's creative and critical thinking. Dewey in the 1930s was promoting a view of education which was based on following or leading learners to their 'big ideas' so that these would form the content of education and be rooted in meaningful and relevant experiences. He was dedicated to ensuring that children and adults had a desire and enjoyment for learning, all the time, and that it was an exciting and affirming experience which would inspire and engage them both intellectually and emotionally. The Reggio Emilia Pre-schools have based their pedagogy on Dewey's philosophy, where children's ideas and creative thinking form the basis for learning and teaching. This is evident in the way that all children are viewed as competent, capable and creative thinkers and learners with huge potential. Their ideas lead what happens in the settings and form the emergent planning, which grows out of the weaving together of children's and adult's interests. In Reggio terms, this is called 'co-constructed creativity' where ideas have been created and connected to other thoughts and materials and as a result new ideas and thinking have been built.

Other ways of viewing and respecting children's ideas are encompassed in the following:

- **Hatching ideas** – Bruce (2004) refers to children and adults 'hatching ideas' as part of their creative repertoire as they play, talk and explore.

- **Fascinations** – Where children are interested and curious about something (an idea) and become captivated and absorbed by it.

- **Having an interest** – Means that all children, including babies and toddlers are capable of initiating their own thoughts and ideas for thinking and learning.

CASE STUDY – Natalia likes to hide in boxes

We can see several ideas unfolding as Natalia plays outside and takes an interest in the bread crates after watching the other children hiding underneath them. She realises, after trying out her first idea, that she is too tall to fit underneath one crate, so she goes to fetch another one and pulls it on top of her like a lid **(pic 1)**. Natalia is not satisfied with this idea, as she can't curl up small enough in the box so that she is totally enclosed **(pic 2)**. Another idea she thinks of is to try the crates standing upright and to ask an adult to hold them together whilst she is inside **(pic 3)** but this still isn't working for her, so she tries to hold them together herself to test out her idea **(pic 4)**.

Then she has another idea and takes this forward with the adult and other children watching and joining in to help when she needs it. Natalia fetches another crate and decides to put it on top of the other two to hold them together and for good measure she finds another to hold it all down and checks that her idea is working **(pic 6)**.

By now, many of the other children are curious and want to see what Natalia is doing, they take an interest in her idea and want to help. They are curious and want to contribute to the idea. Playing with the idea of hiding in the boxes has taken some time, but Natalia is still not satisfied as she hasn't been able to fully envelop or hide herself in the crates. She changes her thinking and has another idea which involves looking for a bigger container to hide in. She finds the red cone-shaped seat, turns it upside down and hides herself inside perfectly **(pic 8)**.

Links to practice

- Observe some of the children you are supporting and look for their unfolding ideas as they play. What might their next steps be and how could you support them to develop her creativity and critical thinking?

Pause for thought

As you read about Natalia and follow the pictures of her unfolding ideas, reflect on what you saw happening during the play with the crates. What does Natalia's idea tell you about her as a creative thinker? What do you think she is learning about?

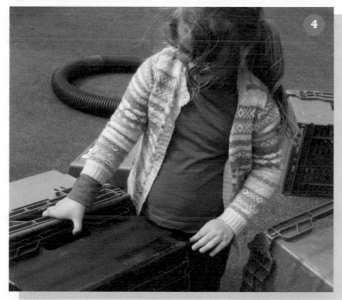

Chapter 2: Children have their own ideas

- **Spontaneous wonderings** – Donaldson (1982) pointed out that part of children's learning is about wondering which arises from 'in the moment experiences'.

- **Possibility thinking** – Craft (2012) explains that children move from a point of 'what if'? (playing with ideas) to 'what can I do with this?' (developing ideas) which is a creative process that involves the imagination, thinking skills and thinking critically.

All these wonderful ways of describing children having their own ideas, have creative qualities of their own including excitement and imagination. They also value and respect who children are, what they think and how they learn. If, as practitioners and teachers, we start at this point, by hooking into children's ideas, interests and fascinations, we have already begun to support children's creativity and critical thinking.

Observing babies, toddlers and young children

One of the best ways to recognise, understand and support children's ideas is to observe them as they are engaged in their play and activities. Watching children's unfolding ideas and their curiosity to understand and make sense of everything is a real privilege and is fundamental to the role of the adult. How can we support and develop children's learning if we don't understand (or attempt to understand) their ideas, their questions, their curiosity? Mary Jane Drummond has skilfully expressed this view in the following statement:

> '*When we work with children, when we play and experiment and talk with them, when we watch them and everything they do, we are witnessing a fascinating and inspiring process: we are seeing them learn. Through our observations in everyday practice we think about what we see, and try to understand it … and then put our understanding to good use*' (Mary Jane Drummond, p.13, 1993).

The process of observation, watching children whilst they are engaged in their play and activities, provides us with a window into their world. So as we watch, we need to take note of what they say (for babies this may be gurgling or babbling), tones of voice, facial expressions, hand movements, body posture, who they are with, how they may be feeling, what they are actually doing and other signals that tell us the story of what is happening. From this rich information we can think about what we have seen and try to understand it. This is not an easy process, but it is one that will bring many surprises and a real joy of working with children – as you never quite know what will happen next! It is, however, a central and crucial part of working with babies, toddlers and young children.

The process of thinking about what you have seen and trying to understand it becomes much easier if you have a good knowledge and understanding of children's development and if you understand the ways in which children learn or the **how** of learning. This means developing your understanding of the three Characteristics of Learning – Play and exploration, Active learning and Creating and thinking critically. There other helpful tools which can be used to interpret and understand what you have observed:

- **Levels of involvement and well-being** (Ferre Laevers, 1994)

- **Schema** – repeatable pattern of thinking which can be observed in children's play

- **Dispositions and attitudes** – how children become interested, excited and motivated about their learning

- **Interests and fascinations** – how children can lead and steer their own thinking and learning.

As you use these tools to understand and interpret what you have seen, you are involved in 'untangling the bowl of spaghetti' that was referred to at the beginning of Chapter 1. The role of the adult, practitioner and teacher, is to make sense of what you have seen, to untangle it and then put it to good use. This means making sure that the next steps or possibilities for those children are firmly built on their current thinking and learning so that future learning is scaffolded.

What we see when we observe very much depends on how open and ready we are. If you watch children with an open mind at various moments of their play and activities and record this, using a camera or video etc. then you will capture the story of their unfolding ideas. This will tell you a great deal about the child's thinking, learning and development.

However, if your observations are infrequent and mainly based on finding out if a child has achieved some specific goal or outcome you will miss the wealth of thinking and learning that is going on; see thinking and learning completely out of context and

AN OBSERVATION OF AAKIFAH AND DANIELA – Playing with leeks

The toddlers in the two-year-old room had been looking at vegetables and cutting them into pieces when Aakifah took a deeper interest in the leeks she had been slicing as she was able to make a lovely cone shape!

Aakifah was interested in the rings of leeks which came apart after she had chopped the leek. She kept putting her finger in the middle of the leek.

Aakifah picked up another' whole piece of leek and again poked her finger in the middle. As she did the rings of the leek extended out in a cone shape on her finger. She held it very carefully and was really pleased with the results.

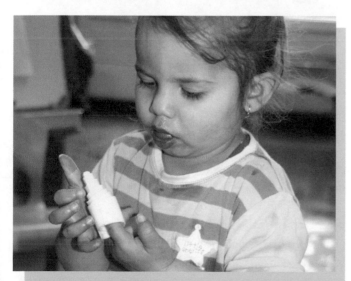

Daniela had been watching Aakifah and liked her idea so came across to have a go herself. With great concentration she put the leek on her finger and pushed the leek with her other hand. It 'concertinaed out' to her great delight.

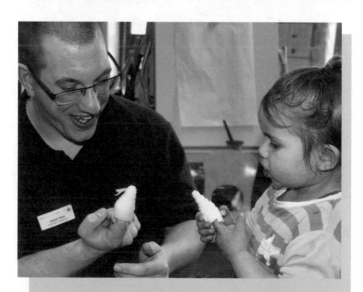

She showed David how to make the leek concertina and they talked together about what had happened; sharing the experience as well as the idea.

very often see what you expect to see. In this way, observation becomes a tool for 'ticking off' arbitrary goals rather than a way of representing the 'story' or narrative of children's unfolding ideas, thinking and learning. The latter gives us a much deeper view of children's progress and development whist the former leads to an overuse of tick sheets and unnecessary paperwork.

What did we see?

Aakifah had an idea after spending some time chopping the vegetables and feeling them. She had been carefully inspecting each of the vegetables but was particularly interested in the shape and smell of the leek as it was a bit more flexible than the others. It took her a few attempts but she could see that by pushing the middle she could change the shape of the leek into this interesting cone which hid her finger. Her curiosity and involvement was evident in her facial expression and the squeals of surprise and delight she made. She experimented with her idea and tried it out several times, occasionally looking up at the adult and saying 'look'. Daniela had been watching Aakifah and was curious about the leek she wanted to try the same thing so had a go and focused very intently on getting her finger in the right place and making the leek spread out. Then she shared this with David who also copied what she was doing so the idea spread.

Future possibilities

Aakifah and Daniela's next steps need to build on the play with the leeks and vegetables and develop conversational talk – so possibilities could include:

- Making soup from the vegetables and tasting them

- Talking about the soup and telling the other children about the leeks and other vegetables

- Sharing the learning story together and with the families

- Reading stories and singing rhymes about food and vegetables e.g. *The enormous turnip*, *Five fat peas*

- Looking for other ways and other equipment which is enveloped e.g. Russian dolls, stacking boxes (you can find some good ones in card shops).

The observation of Aakifah and Daniela shows how children's ideas can happen at any time and anywhere, they are not

Jessica is fascinated with the cloth bag and looking inside it. She also likes to look inside other things like the black reel and boxes. She is beginning to put things inside the bags and boxes and keeps repeating this as she plays, especially with the treasure basket.

She has an enclosure schema, which is developing as she practices, repeats and explores the materials.

necessarily things you can plan for but arise out of good provision and practice with supportive adults who recognise and share in the idea together as David did. For toddlers and babies their earliest forms of ideas can be seen in their schematic play, for example when they continually look for ways to contain things or envelop themselves in blankets, boxes or small spaces. These schematic ideas arise out of an inner need to follow and repeat patterns of play and can become increasingly more complex and sophisticated with the support of adults who know how to extend and develop the child's interest.

Older children's ideas will build on these earlier experiences and become more sophisticated – especially if they have been recognised and encouraged when they were younger. We can see this clearly happening with Natalia and her ideas about the crates.

What is interesting here, is that Natalia's idea is shared by many other children as they all become interested in what she is doing. They come to have look and watch and then, as Daniela did with the leek, they join in.

Bruce (2004) recognises the importance of shared ideas for children's thinking and learning. She calls it 'group creativity' which is about children being part of a group but with opportunities for being an individual within the group on the child's terms.

Group creativity and individual creativity

It is particularly important to focus on group creativity, especially if we want children to engage in talk and discussion; they have to have someone to talk with, to share ideas, thoughts and conversations. Children do have a natural affinity to play with others and make friendships, but we frequently see children in isolation, for example babies are often positioned away from each other in case they fall or injure each other in some way but this means that they have no-one to interact with or bounce ideas off. We also tend to observe children individually rather than several children together which will not tell us about the interaction between them, the shared thinking and how they collaborated together.

Group creativity is the catalyst for sustained shared thinking, where ideas are tossed around in play and activities, taking on new forms, reconstructed and tried out then left to be revived another day. Children's collaborative thinking is an instrumental part of the practice in Reggio Emilia pre-schools. It begins very early on when the children are babies, where they are always sat together, usually in pairs and frequently so they are facing each other toe-to-toe with a single object to provoke the play. In this way they can communicate with each other through passing the object, or touching each other or creating some other idea.

As the children get older these early collaborations have set the foundations for later group creativity to amazing effect. As a result we see a much deeper level of thinking, ideas which are truly creative like 'shadowiness', 'mobility of expression (which included what it means to talk and think), the fountain; and conversational language which is reflective and thoughtful. For example, Anna who is five to six-years-old talks with her friends and the teachers in the Villetta Pre-school about what it is like to work and play in a group,

> *'Because your brain works better. Because your ideas, when you say them out loud, they keep coming together, and when all the ideas come together you get a gigantic idea! You can think better in a group'* (Giudici, C. et al., p.323, 2001).

What Anna is explaining and describing here is the way a group of children (and adults) become much more creative and critical thinkers when they are in a learning community or a group.

However both 'group creativity' and 'individual creativity' (Bruce, 2004) need to grow out of experiences where children feel confident, capable and strong about themselves, their ideas and know they are being listened to. They need to feel emotionally safe 'to go on creative adventures of their own' (Bruce, p.15, 2004). There are strong connections between children's creative and critical thinking and their self-esteem, confidence and well-being. This is not surprising if you consider that children, and adults, need to feel safe and secure in order to feel comfortable and at ease to try something out, make mistakes and feel okay if it all goes wrong. If children are to feel enthusiastic about developing and sharing their ideas with others they need to know that they will be valued and not dismissed.

Four foundations

The theory of creativity and critical thinking has strengthened the connections between creative thought and social and emotional development. For example, the work of Fumoto et al. (p.25, 2012) has emphasised that young children's creativity and critical thinking needs four foundations in order to develop:

Social foundations – Where babies, toddlers and young children need positive well-supported relationships with other children and adults out of which grow friendships and the confidence to collaborate together.

Cognitive foundations – Where babies, toddlers and young children are immersed in opportunities to play with their ideas and develop the dispositions and skills they need to be creative thinkers.

Emotional foundations – Where the well-being of babies, toddlers and young children are fostered and supported including the development of self-confidence, self-esteem and feeling positive about themselves and others.

Motivational foundations – Where babies, toddlers and young children feel intrinsically motivated to 'have a go' and 'try things out' because they want to rather than doing it for a reward like a sticker or a smiley face. This gives them a real feeling of achievement and raises self-esteem and well-being.

Chapter 2: Children have their own ideas

Mindsets

Another way of looking at the relationship between creativity and creative thinking and the social and emotional development of young children, is through the work of Carol Dweck (2006) on 'mindsets'. Mindsets are about how we make judgements of ourselves and others as thinkers and learners, which can happen very early on in life, and as a consequence affect the way in which we develop and progress. So a 'growth mindset' would be where children (and adults) see themselves as competent and capable thinkers and learners, with worthwhile ideas that they are keen to explore, experiment and problem-solve either on their own or with others. In this scenario, children will see themselves as active agents in the learning process with endless potential and exciting prospects for learning.

However, the opposite of this would be a 'fixed mindset' where children (and adults) do not see themselves as thinkers and learners. They will wait for others to tell them what to do and how to do it and that there is always a right answer, which will ultimately lead to a lack of self-confidence and the courage and inclination to have a go and try things for themselves. In this case children will often be passive, unsure of themselves and lack the confidence to try things out, They will worry about getting it wrong to such an extent that they will not even embark on the challenge. Clearly we would want all our children to have a growth mindset and feel they can take on any creative challenge including the expression and development of their own ideas and interests.

Things to look for when observing

There are many things to look out for when you are observing children and their ideas. This is why using photographs, taken in a quick sequence, can help you see some of the detail which you may have missed as it all happened so quickly. It is the interpretation of this, or the untangling, which requires your detective work to make sense of what you have seen the child/children do – including what they may have been thinking.

Remember to think about the child's development, levels of involvement, well-being, schema, dispositions and attitudes, interests and fascinations. The more you observe the more this will make sense to you with the added bonus that your knowledge and skills will develop along the way.

As you become more skilled, you will be able to see the way in which children are self-regulating their thinking and

learning, their possibility thinking, and importantly, evidence of growth mindsets.

Following children's ideas and interests

Another way of viewing the **ideas** that babies, toddlers and young children have is through their **interests** and what they are interested in. This can be thought of in the following way.

thoughts/thinking   beliefs

philosophies/theories

dreams   concepts

IDEAS

feelings   plans/aims

understanding   opinions

curiosity   awareness

involvement

attraction

fascinations

INTERESTS

connections

importance

concentration

attention   enjoyment

These are all characteristics of children's creativity and critical thinking which we would want to promote with a natural connection between the two. We want children to have ideas and interests because this is how they make their thinking visible to the people around them. Ideas and interests are how children represent their thinking; it is who they are and an important part of them. If we don't recognise and listen to their ideas and interests it is like a form of rejection; they should be one of our main points of contact with children's creativity and creative thinking:

'Children actively drive their own learning and development, by the choices they make, the interests they develop, the questions they ask, the knowledge they seek, and their motivation to act more competently' (DCSF, p.6, 2009).

We can see this happening with Blake, who at four-years-old is showing a deep interest in the properties of water particularly around puddles, rivers, the flow of water, machines, movement and mixing. He is driving his learning by asking some very philosophical questions, posing his hypotheses and trying his ideas out as he plays in the water tray at nursery and the outdoor area.

Blake is taking control of his own learning through following his ideas and making suggestions and hypotheses, then trying them out to see what happens. As he does this, he becomes a real 'water expert' and is quite happy to let the other children join in with his interest. His teacher made many observations of his interest, taking pictures and recording the journey of his thinking and learning as it progressed; when she 'untangled' all of the information she found that Blake was working beyond developmental expectations for his age. His conversational language was imaginative, complex and provoked much discussion with other children and adults.

Following children's interests and letting ideas develop supports children's critical thinking and leads to deeper levels of learning and involvement. As they become more absorbed in the interest, children concentrate for longer periods, they stick at it and persist even when it starts to get tough and complicated, they interact more and use imaginative language and they are more likely to collaborate with others and engage in group creativity. Creative thinking is deepened, going beyond the superficial into real depths of finding out, researching and problem solving. We can see this in Blake's interest, with Natalia and the boxes and Aakifah and Daniella as they investigate the leeks. There is real enthusiasm and enjoyment in finding out, experimenting and learning.

There are also crucial connections here to developing a growth mindset and enabling self-regulation as children determine the path of learning for themselves with supportive adults to guide, support and weave in new ideas and learning. As Whitebread (2011) explains, children's self-regulation is: *"commonly found in child-initiated, playful activities including group problem-solving"*. Which means that we need to provide as many opportunities for children's ideas and interests to lead the learning, rather than overly structured and excessive

planning by the adult – that is if we want real, meaningful creative thinking and learning to happen.

By following children's interests, we are more focused on the unfolding ideas and the narrative or story of what the child/children are thinking and the creative process they are engaged in. It's important to see the whole picture and not snapshots as we run the risk of missing something crucial to the *story*. Taking a sequence of photographs or making a short piece of film helps with this, as well as taking notes; then comparing them with other recent observations and pictures to make the connection between what happened before and what came after. Often there is an important pattern or connection which we miss and which could be the missing piece of the puzzle. Many of the observations in this book are all based on narratives or sequences which tell the story of the child's/children's unfolding ideas and interests.

"I can make circles, it goes in, in the middle and out at the edges. It's a water roundabout."

"I am going to make a water machine to make orange juice. It's fizzy, the water will be so fizzy, it will tickle your nose!"

"It isn't a good puddle place, the water runs away; it's a good river place."

"Maybe the puddle was right under the rain cloud."

Chapter 2: Children have their own ideas

Children's interests and adult-led activities – what is the difference?

The Early Years Foundation Stage (EYFS) 2012 framework in England has helpfully made following children's interests or child-initiated activity a statutory requirement for all children; which means that opportunities for this **must** be provided for babies, toddlers and young children in all settings and schools.

> '*Each area of learning and development must be implemented through planned, purposeful play and though a mix of adult-led and child-initiated activity. Play is essential for children's development, building their confidence as they learn to explore, to think about problems, and relate to others. Children learn by leading their own play, and by taking part in play which is guided adults. There is an ongoing judgment to be made by practitioners about the balance between activities led by children, and activities led by or guided by adults. Practitioners must respond to each child's emerging needs and interests, guiding their development through warm, positive interaction.*' (p.6)

This requires a rebalancing of control in the setting or school with adults giving back some space for children's ideas and interests to blossom. The 'balance' is not about a fixed timetable of adult-led activities in the morning and child-led/initiated play in the afternoon, when all the 'work' is completed. The idea of balance, as a weaving together of child and adult-led thinking and learning, rather than a

calculated sharing out of time across the day or week, is much more conducive to supporting children's creativity and critical thinking. This is a partnership or collaboration of learner and teacher who co-construct thinking and ideas together in an inspirational and creative way. The example of building creative thinking together with Emily and the frost, in Chapter 1, shows how the child's interest and the adult-led support can be woven together in one small opportunity that arose without any formal planning. Interestingly, research has shown that opportunities such as this happen more often in '*freely chosen play activities which provide the best opportunities for adults to extend children's thinking*' (REPEY, p.12, 2002). The same research also made clear that when children's ideas and interests were followed and developed together, with a supportive adult, in a process of co-construction, children became involved in sustained shared thinking which is where most thinking and learning happened.

This process of weaving children's ideas and interests together, with adult support and teaching, is quite complicated as it requires a good understanding of children's development and the central role of play in their lives. It also relies on adults being able to recognise these significant moments as children play and then know when to join in and scaffold the learning. These things can only happen if the adults have given children the space and time to do this and they observe what is occurring in front of them. The reward is a truly meaningful experience for children (including babies and toddlers), that respects their innate ideas and curiosity and views them as competent and creative thinkers. It is also one of the real joys of working with young children as we witness the unfolding of children's thinking and learning:

> '*Watch (children's) interest…listen to their questions…then you will not be able to doubt the strength and spontaneity of their wish to know and understand*' Susan Isaacs (Rich et al., p.25, 2005).

The parallel characteristics to creating and thinking critically – which are play and exploration and active learning, all weave together to support this complex process of children's learning and development (Moylett, 2012, McTavish, 2012).

Adult support

It is the adults that babies, toddlers and young children meet and build relationships with, as well as their parents and families, who will have the biggest role to play in nurturing them as creative and critical thinkers and leaners. Adults need to be curious and open-minded about children, adopting a 'detective' like approach to watching and understanding what they say and do and never taking anything for granted. In this way they can do what Claxton recommends: 'help children to discover what they want to be passionate about' (2009).

There are many dimensions to this role, some of which are included in each of the chapters in this book. Of course we don't do all these things separately and at different times as they are all part of the rich repertoire of the adult's working with babies, toddlers and young children. Each aspect needs to be seen in the wider context of children's development and learning and are all interlinked and woven together.

Tuning-in to children's ideas

The connections between children's creativity and critical thinking and their social and emotional development have already been made. However, we cannot underestimate children's fundamental need (and right) to be nurtured through good attachment and attunement with the adults who are a significant part of their lives. These are the deep foundations upon which children's future, all round development is constructed.

Attunement is all about the connection the adult has with children and the relationship that is forged from responding to their needs, particularly emotional needs, so that they feel understood and valued. The adult's close relationship with the children comes out of knowing who they are, how they feel and what they are thinking and taking an interest in. Bruce (2004) calls this 'sensitive companionship' (p.25) where the adult has cultivated a relationship that is warm, trusting, affectionate and interested. It is a relationship that says to the children: I am interested in you and what you think. I want to listen to your ideas because I think they are unique, imaginative and inspiring and I am always excited by what you say and do. This acceptance and respect then leads to children feeling emotionally safe and secure (they have a feeling of belonging) to share their inner ideas/thoughts with you, remembering that sometimes children's ideas/thoughts can be challenging both emotionally and cognitively.

Adults will need to be emotionally available, open and in-tune with the signs and signals that children give through their play, their conversation and their feelings; much of which

> **Attunement is all about the connection the adult has with children and the relationship that is forged from responding to their needs, particularly emotional needs, so that they feel understood and valued. The adult's close relationship with the children comes out of knowing who they are.**

happens through our on-going observations of children and leads to the following:

> *'Adults who tune into what interests the child and who are informed participant observers are able to appreciate and value the beginning s of creativity in children without invading the child's creative idea or taking it over'* (Bruce, p.25, 2004).

Observation and listening to children's ideas

Observation and listening to children is at the heart of this book, with strands running through every aspect of creating and thinking critically. How are we to know and understand where children are in their complex development from babies to toddlers to young children, as well as make an attempt to unravel what they may be thinking and the ideas they have, if we don't watch them? Good observation can tell us most of what we need to know, but this does mean going beyond the superficial nature of looking out for the arbitrary learning of colours, numbers and shapes.

If we are concerned with the characteristics of children's learning, the **how** of their learning, then we need to be looking for the deeper level dispositions such as concentration, involvement and imagination, as well as the development of ideas, the connections that children make and the ways they decide to implement their creative ideas and thinking.

Observation is a way of listening to children. The term 'listening' is used in a much broader way here and includes listening to what children say, their conversations and language. However, it also means listening to their ideas and thinking, listening to their feelings and emotions, listening to their physical movements and body posture, listening to their facial expressions, listening to their imagination and excitement, listening to their fears, worries, joys and excitement. In effect, it means being open-minded about what the children 'bring' and being aware of the many different ways they communicate who they are and what they think. Importantly, this kind of open-minded listening should be leading the way with babies and toddlers, as well as with young children.

Children's conversational language is a significant part of the observations we make as this is another window into their ideas and how they interpret their thinking; as such many more observations should be made which record what children say particularly as part of a conversation with others, children and adults. The following observation of a conversation between Emily (aged four) and her teacher Kath, shows the development of Emily's ideas about the frost with Kath supporting and extending her thinking:

K: Have you seen the grass just here? (Pointing to a frosty patch).
E: Yes it's white and it's cold.
K: Look it's sparkly.
E: Yeh, yeh, look (running around on it).

K: Why do you think it's like that?
E: There is frost on it.
K: Yes.
E: It's really, really cold.
K: Look where I'm standing (on a patch of grass where there is no frost) There isn't any frost here.
E: No, no there isn't.
K: I wonder why that is?
E: Because the frost isn't coming down there.
K: What do you mean?
E: There isn't any frost coming down on it. Out of the sky.
K: Is there frost coming out of the sky where you are?
E: Yes.
K: Is that where the frost comes from?
E: Yes look (reaching up with both hands and looking up to the sky) it's coming down and down and down onto here (crouches down and touches the grass).
K: I can't see it coming down.
E: No.
K: (Standing on a non-frosty part of the grass) Why isn't it coming down here then?
E: Don't know.
K: Look, this part is frosty too and this bit isn't (Both run from place to place in the garden looking at where the frost is).

They both continue to think about why there is frost on one part of the grass and not the other. This involves a great deal of talk about shadows and sunshine.

Narrative observations

Most of the observations in this book are narrative observations, which tell the story of the child/children's unfolding ideas and thinking. This is much more helpful than doing snapshot observations as they will tell you much more about the children's deeper levels of thinking and learning and you will see the connections they are making. In effect, you will be saving a lot of time as the narrative observation will give a much more detailed picture of the child/children's development. A narrative observation can be used in so many different ways:

- As a 'story' of what the children have been doing which can be read back to them so that they can reflect on what they have done and add further ideas/comments.

- It can be turned into the child's/children's book which can be shared with other children and taken home to read together with the family.

- It can be used with parents to explain the 'story' behind their child's play, what they were saying and thinking. Parents will see their child's development and learning in context and be able to support this a home by doing similar things.

- It can be used as a display to document the unfolding ideas and thinking of the child/children with added notes from the adults to make links to assessment and further planning.

- They can form a collection of evidence of the progress children have made whilst they were at the setting/school.

Reviewing or making sense of what you have seen has been discussed earlier in this chapter, but think of this as a point at which you need to delve into your observation tool kit in order to interpret as accurately as you can what the child/children have done and how this has supported and developed their thinking and learning. By using this range of tools we can be as objective and clear as possible in the decisions we make about children's learning and their progress. However, achieving total objectivity in our evaluations is not possible as there will always be an element of subjectivity based on the decisions you make; the important thing is that they are informed decisions based on your professional judgement.

There are various other tools available which can help us to understand what we see and inform our decisions; one of which is the observation-led Analysing Children's Creative Thinking (ACCT) Framework designed as part of the Froebal Research Fellowship project 'The voice of the child; Ownership and Autonomy in Early Learning' (Fumoto, p.3, 2012). The framework identifies many aspects that characterise children's creative thinking and what these look like when we are observing and analysing what we have seen. The table overleaf outlines the 'indicators for creative thinking' which, when pieced together, give a rich picture of children's thinking (Fumoto et al., p.95, 2012).

Have a look at this table on page 40 which explains some of the observable aspects of children's creative thinking.

Using a tool like this helps not only to interpret what we see children doing when we watch them but it also tells us what they are not doing and importantly tells us what opportunities and experiences we need to provide in the setting/school to enable this to happen. Observation isn't just about what the children are doing it also forms part of our quality 'control' in terms of practice and provision.

Links to practice

Discuss these 'indicators for creative thinking' with other members of your team and think about what they might look like when you observe babies, toddlers and young children. Through your shared discussion and thinking you will be able to understand how these indicators contribute to children's creative thinking and learning.

We are making observations of children all the time as we play, interact and engage with them; some of these will be quick 'in the moment' observations which then inform how we respond to an action, question or a comment. Often we do this without really being aware of the quick decisions we are making and it is part of the skill of the adult to observe, wait, and listen before deciding what to do next to support the child/children. Standing back and scanning the engagement of the child/children as they develop their ideas and thinking through their play enable adults to 'choose wisely when to step in to provoke, clarify, support, extend, challenge' (Craft. A, p.50, 2012). In this way on going observation forms one of the main strategies we use to support and develop children's thinking and learning in a process of co-construction.

Chapter 2: Children have their own ideas

Indicators for creative thinking – look for these as you observe children

Indicator	What does this mean	What does this look like in practice? (Fill in below)
EXPLORATION		
Exploring	Child is keen to explore, and/or shows interest in the potential of a material or activity.	
Engaging in new activity	Child is interested in becoming involved in an activity and taking an idea forward. The activity could be of his/her own choice or suggested by another child or adult.	
Knowing what you want to do	Child shows enjoyment or curiosity when choosing to engage in an activity.	
INVOLVEMENT AND ENJOYMENT		
Trying out	Child shows evidence of novel ways of looking and planning: uses prior knowledge or acquires new knowledge to imagine and/or hypothesise, or to show flexibility and originality in his/her thinking.	
Analysing ideas	Child shows either verbal or behavioural evidence of weighing up his/her idea, and deciding whether or not to pursue it.	
Speculating	Child makes a speculative statement or asks a question of him/herself, or of other children or adults, relating to the activity.	
Involving others	Child engages with one or more children or adults to develop an idea or activity: may articulate an idea, seek to persuade others, or show receptivity to the ideas of others.	
PERSISTANCE		
Persisting	Child shows resilience, and maintains involvement in an activity in the face of difficulty, challenge or uncertainty. He/she tolerates ambiguity.	
Risk taking	Child displays a willingness to take risks, and to learn from mistakes.	
Completing challenges	Child shows a sense of self-efficacy, self-belief and pleasure in achievement: shows conscious awareness of his/her own thinking.	

Supporting and co-constructing children's ideas

The adult who is tuned-in to children's ideas and thinking, observes them whilst they are in the midst of their play and activities and as their sensitive companion will, most likely, be involved in the co-construction of learning, since they are already aware of what interests the child/children are following and are eager to support them further. We saw an example of co-construction or building thinking together, in Chapter 1 with Emily and the frosty day, and we can see it happening with the group of children playing with the crates in this chapter.

Adults need to think about how they can build and extend children's thinking, their ideas and their conversational language without 'dropping the ball'. This process, called co-construction or scaffolding, involves listening/observing the child/children whilst they are in the midst of their play or activity and thinking about how you intervene, what you say and do. Often you are making these decisions in the blink of an eye but the more you do it the better you become at making the right decisions. It's helpful to have a bank of possibility questions in your head that you can use spontaneously in response to the children e.g. 'what do you think?' , 'I wonder if…?', 'what does that remind you of…?', 'can you remember…?'. If you can't remember them, put some up around the setting so that everyone can be aware of possibility questions to extend creative thinking.

Co-construction also happens when you are part of the play, so being in the middle of it is a good place to be, not as the adult in charge but as a sensitive companion or playful partner; where you take on a role or play alongside mirroring what the children are doing. Craft calls this 'meddling in the middle' (p.58, 2012) which means taking your cues and following the child/children's lead, repeating or reflecting back what they have said, making a commentary of what they are doing or standing back and adding thought-provoking language or materials – provocations. The adult would be using a mixture of these strategies in order to keep the play going and extend it further into sustained shared thinking (Chapter 4).

The enabling environment

The enabling environment has a significant part to play in the development of children's creative ideas and critical thinking. Babies, toddlers and young children need an environment and

opportunities, which not only support the ideas they already have, but also spark other fascinations and interests. That means that the environment needs to be open to possibilities with materials that are creative, inspiring and open-ended. This is a good checklist to keep in your head when thinking about the materials/equipment you provide for all children. For example, a pop-up toy will hold an interest for short amount of time and then become uninspiring where as a small cardboard box and a wooden spoon dressed in various ways, which you and the child can pop-up, will lead to endless opportunities for surprise, curiosity, laughter, talking and singing. If we want children to be creative and critical thinkers, we have to be creative and critical thinkers.

Playing with ideas

Play is probably the best forum for children to create, grow and think about their ideas. It isn't a coincidence that play is a child's main occupation for every minute they are awake and active; it is there to fulfil their innate and spontaneous desire to find out, explore and develop their thinking. It is one of the fundamental ways in which babies, toddlers and young children make their ideas visible to us. How is a child to express the complexities of their thinking if they cannot communicate this through play or language? As babies grow into toddlers and young children they are able to express their ideas and thinking in other, additional ways like painting, drawing, modelling, singing and stories, but play and conversational talk remain

the key translator of young children's thinking. Play provides children with the opportunity to think out loud.

The opportunities that are provided for play need to tap into this desire to follow ideas and interests and the co-construction of thinking and learning. There is a real harmony between the creativeness of play and the creativeness of children's ideas; they support each other and create perfect conditions for critical thinking as long as the play is open-ended, flexible and balanced, with the child/children leading the way (child-initiated play) sometimes and the adult leading it at others (adult-led/focused).

Enabling play environments which support the development of children's ideas will have continuous provision which consists of carefully chosen open-ended materials which have the potential to be anything the child wants it to be. The 'less is more' philosophy is a helpful one to remember as it is better to have sufficient amounts of one type of material or pieces of equipment than to have so many different ones that children become frustrated when there isn't enough to go around or complete an idea. Equally, it is more productive to invest in high quality materials like hollow blocks and wooden bricks so that they are appealing and robust. Continuous provision should be enhanced on the basis of children's growing ideas to support them and to provoke further creative thinking.

Playing with ideas also means that children need to feel able to try things out, experiment and 'take risks'. There will be

times when it all goes wrong, and ideas fall apart, but this is all part of the process of learning and strongly connected to problem solving. Children need to know that it is okay to get it wrong and try again so that they feel strong enough to keep on trying and persist with something until they are satisfied. If they give up or feel afraid of getting things wrong, children will never trust in taking a chance again and lose that important development of a growth mindset.

Time for ideas to develop

Having the time to develop ideas is a further aspect to consider in providing an enabling environment for ideas. It takes time to play with an idea, look for solutions, refine it, try it out and share it with others so adults need to ensure that the structure of the routines do not overly interrupt children's thinking or hurry them along. As well as the view of children as 'hatchers' of ideas, Bruce (2004) points out that children need time to 'incubate ideas', which means taking time to refine and rethink (simmering) as well as trying it out and growing your idea with others.

If children are in an environment which is overly formal and structured with the adult in control, at all times these crucial opportunities and experiences will not happen. A 'stop-start' routine where children are frequently interrupted for adult-led activities like, group snack time, phonics sessions and PE will lead to them realising that that there is no point in starting any

Links to practice

Does the enabling environment in your setting/school provide opportunities for children to play with their ideas, take risks and make mistakes and have the time to incubate and hatch ideas?

Are the materials you provide open to possibilities? Are they creative, inspiring and open-ended?

Stand back and observe the children, listen to their thinking and ask yourself these questions. Discuss what you see and think with other members of the team. Is there anything you need to change?

idea or thinking as they will have to stop. As a result, children will become overly dependent on the adult to tell them what to do, concentration will be fleeting and they will not become engrossed in their learning. If we want children to regulate their own learning and be autonomous, then having time to follow your thinking through is essential.

Communication and language

Children's thoughts, ideas and interests are made visible through their communication and language. We can see this in the imaginative and scientific way that Blake articulated his thoughts about the water and then tried them out to test his hypotheses.

The conversation with Emily and the adult shows how talking together can develop and extend an idea, as well as confirm and clarify thinking. The collaborative play with the crates involved many children, over a long period of time, talking with each other and the adult to find ways to fit into the spaces and hide. This group of children also communicated their ideas by watching what each other was doing, copying the idea to take it further and then contributing to the shared idea.

The communication of ideas through watching was also evident with Aakifah and Daniela as they played with the leeks and discovered what would happen if they put their finger in the middle. As Jessica explored the treasure in the treasure basket we could see her ideas being communicated through her focused eyes and inquisitive, curious expression.

Being able to communicate your ideas and thinking at such a young age could be quite a challenge, but children have an incredible collection of tools to help them with this, including: play, watching, copying, experimenting and collaborating. Also, through their dispositions they communicate interest, fascination, excitement, curiosity, frustration and persistence.

All of these 'tools'; dispositions, as well as language and conversational talk, enable children to communicate their creativity and critical thinking. They are all part of the child's 'Hundred Languages'.

> If we want children to regulate their own learning and be autonomous, then having time to follow your thinking through is essential.

Key points

This chapter has looked in depth at what happens when children's ideas are respected, accepted, and supported by the adults around them and how this contributes to the development of creative and critical thinking.

The key points to think about are:

- Children's big ideas

- What children's ideas look like and how they unfold

- Individual creativity and collaborative creativity

- Understanding the theory of creativity and critical thinking – involvement, flow, mind-sets, possibility thinking and self-regulation

- The central role of observation and how we can document children's ideas

- The crucial links between creating and thinking critically and children's self-esteem and emotional well-being

- Adults tuning-in to children's ideas, interests and fascinations and co-constructing or scaffolding the development of thinking

- Children having the time to play with their ideas and experiencing creative, open-ended environments and materials.

Chapter 3:
Children make links

The Early Years Foundation Stage (2008) stressed in the theme of Learning and Development that children's creativity and critical thinking was about making connections, transforming understanding and sustained shared thinking.

Babies, toddlers and young children make connections or links in their thinking as part of the process of their learning and development; it is the linking together of their ideas, experiences and knowledge that supports not just their creativity and critical thinking, but their whole, all round progress.

The process of children making links or connections can be best described as:

'When children have opportunities to play with ideas in different situations and with a variety of resources, they discover connections and come to new and better understandings and ways of doing things. Adult support in this process enhance their ability to think critically and ask questions' (EYFS (2008) Learning and Development Card 4.3).

This chapter will look in much more depth at this process.

Children make links

The use of the words 'link' or 'connection' to describe the process of children piecing together their ideas, experiences and knowledge are interchangeable; they both concern how something is 'joined up', 'attached' or 'brought together', in this case: children's creative and critical thinking.

Think of children's learning and development as a jigsaw puzzle with many pieces; it involves how babies, toddlers and young children begin to make sense of the world around them through testing it out, trying their ideas and adding all of this to what they already know. Gradually the pieces come together and the whole picture becomes much clearer.

Piaget explained this process of development as children 'assimilating' new experiences and information and 'accommodating' it into what they already know and understand. Giovanni, at five-years-old, explains it this way:

> '*For example, when you're with a group you feel like you don't know some things, because you're not an expert, and someone else helps you and that way you learn stuff, like building walls, and the thing you learned sticks inside and it never comes off because it sticks to the other ideas you've already got.*' (Giudici. C, et al., p.326, 2001).

In Chapter 1, Jessica at six-months-old was 'hoovering' up her experiences of the treasure basket and the various materials and containers she was interested in; as she played with the materials she could explore using all her senses, test them out and create ideas and hypotheses about the objects. Her thoughts were coming together as she looked for familiar patterns, searched out new ideas and made connections, rather like a scientist would experiment and test out theories.

As the connections are made Jessica will develop an increasing awareness of the world around her and the people, places and things in that world; she will become a competent and capable thinker and learner.

Gopnick et al. (1999) have written extensively on the powerful, creative thinking undertaken by babies and toddlers and have promoted the view of children as scientists when they are engaged in understanding what is happening around them by 'testing hypotheses, seeking explanations and formulating new theories'. This in itself is a powerful, creative process and one that involves much critical thinking, leading to the creation of new possibilities, new thinking and new ideas.

Schematic interests

The earliest patterns and connections we see in babies' and toddler's critical thinking are through their schematic interests, for example, as they explore trajectories by dropping objects and waiting until someone picks it up for them and as they enjoy rolling balls in lines and singing rhymes which involve jumping up and down.

Jessica shows a schematic interest in enclosure as she peeps inside things like the bag and the cotton reel, and likes to gather small objects and put them in bags.

These are all early ideas which, when connected together form patterns of thinking or schema which are repeated in various situations; developed as long as they are supported by the adults and environment around them; and transferred to new experiences and possibilities.

Leo's story overleaf illustrates these points very well. As his play unfolds, we can see in the observation, the connections he is making and the testing out of his ideas. Its also important to think about what might happen next.

CASE STUDY – Leo's story

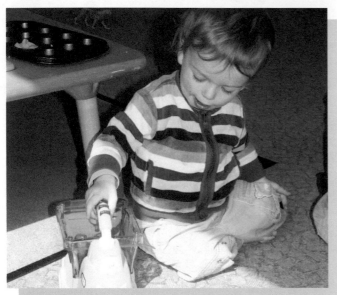

Leo was playing with the rolling truck moving it backwards and forwards over and over again. He didn't say anything but his face was focused on the wheels with a serious expression and concentration.

He stood up and carefully started to push the truck further along around the room, gathering up speed and using the truck for support as well as checking out the route he could take.

Leo zoomed around with the truck with a sense of purpose, then stopped, looked across the room into the corner and had an idea. He went off with the truck carrying it into the corner. His idea was to fetch another truck, which he knew was in the corner of the room.

He had one in each hand and started to push them together in front of him. This was a bit more of a challenge than pushing one truck! He levelled up the trucks to give him more balance and with real concentration, tongue out, and careful precision he transported the two trucks forwards and back across the room, looking for more space.

What did we see?

Leo has been toddling confidently for a few weeks and is steadier on his feet; he really likes to push something along and particularly likes the pram and the trucks. He had an idea a few days ago to use two trucks together and keeps practicing this, getting more proficient and confident at keeping the trucks in line and pushing them along. He suddenly seems to have an idea, you can see this in his face through his expression, and then he is on a mission to find what he needs and follow it through. He becomes very involved in this and spends up to 15 minutes concentrating, being absorbed and not easily distracted. It seems like all his energy goes on this and he doesn't say very much at all but you can see him communicating his ideas through his actions and facial expression. We think Leo has a trajectory and transporting schema as we have seen this frequently in his play – he also likes to push the pram.

Further possibilities for Leo?

We need to follow Leo's interest in trajectories and transporting, so we could try the following with him:

- Rolling balls down guttering or drain pipes

- Using the wind-up cars and trains to provoke more interest and ideas

- Use larger sit on trucks outside for Leo to push along with his legs and feet.

We also need to encourage Leo to talk about his ideas and express his thoughts, so we could try the following:

- Model possible language whilst playing alongside Leo and making a commentary on what he is doing

- Show Leo his story of the trucks and 'read' it to him. Listen to his responses and record what he says

- Sing some action rhymes with him that have up and down movements e.g. incey, wincy, spider.

Learning and development

Children's learning continues to grow and develop through this process of piecing together new experiences and information

Pause for thought

Take some time to think about the paragraph above and the implications for children's thinking, learning and development. What would happen to children's creative thinking if they did not have these rich and appropriate experiences?

Links to practice

Think about the kinds of experiences that would be appropriate for babies, toddlers and young children and the potential they have for children to think and be creative and make connections.

and linking it to their existing understanding. All of which depends on them having a range of rich and appropriate experiences, with adults who can support and guide, rather than do it for them or hurry them along. They also need plenty of time to weave all this thinking together, absorb it and transform it into something new.

In the early years (birth-7) children's learning and development is at its most rapid and most complicated, there is so much to learn and make sense of – which makes it absolutely crucial that these early encounters with learning are truly understood and mastered before progressing on to the next. It is all about firm foundations and becoming a resilient, skilled thinker and learner who can feel confident about taking on new challenges with eagerness and enjoyment. Being a creative and critical thinker is a messy business in that children's thinking is tangled and woven together like the bowl of spaghetti that Malaguzzi describes. There are no neat beginnings, middle and ends – neither should there be – this is what makes children's thinking creative and unique.

The 'tangle' is about the holistic way in which children learn and develop (this actually applies to the way we all think and learn) and the importance of adults recognising and accepting that learning needs to be holistic if children are to make their own connections and then come to understand the world around them. For example, if we reflect back on the observation

Chapter 3: Children make links

Pause for thought

Scenario 1:

A group of 20 children (aged 4-5 yrs) are sat with the adult on the carpet for a phonics session, which will last for 30 minutes. They are looking at the initial sounds of 'c' and 'p' with the adult holding up the letters and telling the children about the sounds, the children have to repeat the sounds that the adult makes and draw the shape of the letters in the air with their fingers. The adult shows them some pictures that begin with the letters – cat, cucumber, polar bear and pea. The adult asks the children if they can think of some other words that begin with 'c' and 'p'. After the activity has finished the children can go and choose from a range of other provision which has been set out which consists of plastic letters in the water tray and sand, jigsaws and puzzles with letters, a large floor mat with letters and some photocopied sheets with the letters 'c' and 'p' to colour in. The adult leaves the children to play whilst she leads another activity.

Scenario 2:

A small group of 10 children (aged 4-5 yrs) are sat with the adult on the carpet for a phonics session which will last for 20 minutes. They are looking at the initial sounds of 'c' and 'p' with the adult reading *Pat the Cat* (Hawkins, 1995) with them; they read it together as it's a familiar book and the children enjoy the rhyming words. As the words come up the adult writes them underneath each other on a white board: pat… cat…hat…sat…mat…bat… then asks the children if they notice anything. They chatter together and point out the similarities in the words and the differences and can see the connections between the letters 'at'. The adult points out the differences in the initial letter and the sounds of 'c' and 'p' and she brings out a tray of objects some of which begin with these sounds and the children choose an object and talk about it. Afterwards the adult leaves the book, the writing and the objects on the carpet so that the children can continue to play with them.

Throughout the day the adult keeps referring to Pat the Cat, singing rhymes and making up short stories like 'Pat the cat went to the party and what do you think he did?'. The talking and play develop with the children making up their own stories about Pat with the adult following their lead and documenting the action through observation.

Links to practice

Which scenario do you think is more meaningful to the children and why? How do the activities help children to make connections in their thinking and learning? Which scenario do you think enables the children to engage in creative and critical thinking? How does this contribute to the holistic learning of the children?

in Chapter 2 with Aakifah and Daniela exploring the leeks, the evaluation takes a holistic view of their thinking and learning with a focus on their dispositions, involvement and all round development. It views the children's learning from the perspective of **how** they learned and highlights the aspects of their development as thinkers and learners rather than always unpicking **what** they learned, like 'could name the colour of the leek' or 'can hold leek in pincer grip in right hand'. In this way we are able to take a much deeper look at what is actually happening rather than focusing on superficial, easily-measured outcomes.

If we view children's learning and development in this interconnected way then it is much more likely that we will recognise when children are making connections in their learning and we will know how to support these crucial links. We will also see children's thinking and learning in an appropriate and meaningful context which makes sense to them and views the process of the experience/activity as the significant part of learning, rather than the end product.

Experiences that are unconnected may be confusing for children as they could be unsure of how they link to their other experiences and they may even avoid them. For example, many phonics sessions are undertaken as separate 'phonics time' or 'letters and sounds time' with children coming together for a focused, adult-led activity. However, this experience needs to connect children's growing understanding of sounds; letters and words to the wider context of their thinking and learning in a meaningful way, otherwise children may see this as an isolated activity which they have to endure until they can 'go'! These points are illustrated in the scenarios in the Pause for thought box on this page.

The key message here is that children's critical thinking and creativity happen anywhere, at any time and in any area, not just expressive arts and design (DfE, 2012) and creative activities or when you are undertaking a painting or collage. It is also important to remember not to fragment children's potential thinking and learning into easily defined areas, like reading, writing and numeracy, as children don't learn in this way. Chapter 1 explained how young children's thinking and learning was 'tangled' and 'woven together' and not a neat and tidy process, divided into areas of leaning; it is holistic and interconnected. In Scenario 2 the children were not just involved in phonics, they were sharing an enjoyable experience together as a group (PSED), the activity was contributing to their confidence and self-esteem as they became involved and inspired by creating their own rhymes (PSED), their wider experiences were being supported through the introduction of unfamiliar objects (Knowledge of the world), they were able to connect the use of phonics to talking, reading, writing and making up rhymes (CLL), and they were able to develop the rhymes using the whole of their bodies in a physical way outside (PD). The children don't actually need to know that this is what they are doing, as it is the adult's job to untangle what they see before them, document it in some way through observation and make sure that the children are developing in all areas and importantly identify where they need further support.

Sustained shared thinking

Sustained shared thinking is built upon through children either making their own connections in partnership with each other or with the collaborative support of an adult. Either way, the co-construction of learning is formed by connecting what you already know, to new ideas, and transforming this into different and deeper levels of thinking; this is a creative act and involves all the power of critical thinking. Malaguzzi's explanation of the 'table tennis game' in Chapter 1 is a good image of sustained shared thinking to keep in mind when you are involved with the children, including babies and toddlers. Try to keep the ball 'in play' at all times in these situations.

It is all about the sharing of thinking and ideas between each other and building them further, which is why it has to be **shared** and **sustained**. This means that 'doing your thinking together' is going to open up more opportunities for sustained shared thinking in a collaborative way; so group creativity is more likely to generate shared thinking and ideas than individual creativity. We all tend to build our critical thinking and understanding when we are involved in group learning

and can discuss our thinking and ideas; it's called being a community of leaners and is one of the most reflective and productive places to grow your thinking.

If we look at the rest of the conversation (from Chapter 2) between Emily and her teacher (Kath) we can see how skilfully Kath supports her to make connections from what she already knows to new understandings about the frost:

K: Look, this part is frosty too and this bit isn't. (Both of us run from place to place in the garden looking at where the frost is.) Look at your shadow.
E: Yeh, look (runs around).
K: Can you see my shadow?
E: Yes it's there.
K: Can you see any other shadows anywhere? (Trying to draw her attention to the shadows created by the trees).
E: No, there aren't any more.
K: I can see some.
E: Where?
K: Look (pointing to shadow made by a tree with several branches).
E: (excited) Oh yes, that's one isn't it.
K: Whose shadow is that then?
E: I don't know. It isn't anybody's.
K: Where's it coming from then? What's making it?
E: I don't know.
K: Look at these long pointy lines. What do they look like?
E: Like a tree. They're like the branches on a tree.
K: Lets follow this branch and along this straight bit (the shadow of the trunk). Oh we're right up to the trunk (both standing pressed up against the trunk).
E: (laughing with arms round the trunk) let's go back up! (We run up and down the shadow of the trunk several times).
K: Can you see any more tree shadows?
E: Yes there's one right here! (she runs over to another tree's shadow looks around) And one there. (Emily is now able to see the shadows made by the separate trees that she was unable to distinguish before.)

Observation

Observation will help us to see, acknowledge and understand the connections that children are making as they are involved in their play and activities. It will tell the story of what has happened as it unfolds, like in Leo's story where we can see from a series of pictures taken in quick succession how his ideas about moving the truck are developed and the links he makes to what he already knows and understands. If there had only been one picture of Leo and a sticky-note, we would not have understood the deeper meanings of his play or made any connections ourselves to his wider development and learning. By thinking of observation as a story or narrative of what the child is involved in we see the whole picture. Sometimes these observations are called 'learning stories' and have developed from the New Zealand model of observation (Carr, M., 2001) which follows the dispositions of:

- Taking an interest – recognising that the child/children are interested in something, someone or some place. This is often a starting point for children's creative thinking and frequently leads to …

- Being involved – it's usual that when an interest is being followed the child/children become more involved and engaged and will then …

- Persist with difficulty – stick at the play or activity, concentrate and keep trying even if it is hard work and a challenge …

- Express an idea or a feeling – where the child/children communicate in a range of ways (language, gesture, music, art, writing, using numbers and patterns, telling stories) what they are doing, thinking and feeling. All of which usually leads to …

- Taking responsibility – inevitably the child/children have taken ownership of their thinking and learning and are happy to share this with others and collaborate with children and adults …

Observations that follow this learning story-type format are focusing on the holistic nature of children's learning and development as well as focusing on how they are learning and they help the adult to see the connections children are making as their idea/interest develops. In effect, the learning story or narrative is a way of documenting (recording) children's creative thinking and making it visible to share with others including the children; it tells the whole story. In addition these narrative-type observations acknowledge the child's voice and perspective. The learning story on the next page tells what happened when the children played collaboratively on the climbing frame with an adult supporting and extending their ideas.

What did we see?

There was a great deal happening in the play. Diana and Ammar were focused on pulling up the bricks and building the door though they were not playing together. Diana's fascination with pulling up the bricks, the boys interest in filling the bucket and pulling the rope and Ammar's idea of making the door, all worked together whilst being individual actions of play. Children's concentration and involvement was evident in their dedication to the task, their persistence and the extended amount of time they played together. The children were sharing and collaborating both ideas and actions and whilst Ammar became frustrated about the children knocking the door down – this wasn't intentional, they just couldn't get past!

Ammar was focused, concentrating and persisting with his door building – connecting his ideas to the story the day before and playing with a real purpose. Even when he moved away from the door building he had another idea and was eager to use the rope to pull the children up the slide. He didn't say very much – probably because he was so involved in his idea.

Diana has always liked using the pulley and pulling up the bucket – she really wanted to do this on her own but with some persuasion she accepted help from the others. She stuck at the bucket-pulling for over 25 minutes and showed her determination in getting the job done.

Majeed had been watching what was happening and helping with the group of boys to pull up the bucket – then he became involved in pulling the children up the slide and helping Ammar with the task.

Further possibilities

Developing the children's ideas and interests in the climbing frame and pulling play could include:

- Time to repeat and develop the current play on the climbing frame – add more buckets, bricks, rope and a block and tackle.

- Have the tarpaulins and large peg/clamps ready near to the climbing frame.

- Leave books and pictures which show cranes, lifting equipment and rock climbing on a blanket on the grass. Add clip boards, paper, pens and pencils.

CASE STUDY – the climbing frame

A group of children were drawn to the climbing frame and a bucket and pulley system which had been set up by the adult. They were all helping to pull the bucket up to Diana after Ammar had filled it with bricks. There was a great deal of talking and shouting as they all pulled on the rope. "Pull, pull, pull".

Diana was waiting for the bucket and grabbed it as it came towards her. She busily unloaded the bricks and sent the bucket back down again saying "it's empty, we need some more". Ammar was ready with some more bricks to fill the bucket.

Diana carried on waiting for the bricks to be pulled up by the children at the bottom of the rope but Ammar came up to help as he seemed to have an idea about what to use the bricks for. They all carried on lifting the bricks up in the bucket making at least four lifts with everyone helping – shouting directions and getting quite excited about the job.

Ammar started to use the bricks to build a door for the house. He remembered the story they had the other day of 'The three little pigs' and he said the house needs a door to stop 'the big bad wolf' getting in.

CASE STUDY CONTINUED – the climbing frame

He built the bricks upwards and interlocked them to stop them from falling over, then went inside the house to check that it was working and it was a good door. The other children kept getting in the way which made Ammar a bit cross – he kept telling them to move.

He carried on building fetching more bricks from Diana who was still pulling them up in the bucket. Ammar was so absorbed in what he was doing and had to carry on building with lots of noise and children going in and out of the house. He continued to do this by himself for at least 20 mins.

Ammar's door kept getting knocked down as the children went in and out of the house – then Ammar moved on to another idea as rope was being used at the other side of the slide to pull children up. They worked together to pull the children up the slide using the rope.

The children pulled each other up the slide. This was much harder than pulling up the bucket with the bricks as the children were heavy. They had to work out how to do this and negotiate one child at a time. Sue joined in with the idea and made some suggestions as well as giving some support by taking the weight of Alfie so that it was easier to pull him up.

- Share the learning story with the children and ask them to add their comments and thoughts as well as what they think should happen next. Print the story out and add to the display in the nursery – add in other pictures and comments (the child's voice) as they happen.

- Leave the cameras handy for the children so they can take their own pictures.

- Adults to observe again and jot down what the children are saying – use a flip camera to record action and talk.

The pulling, pushing and building play on the climbing frame lasted all morning and had been continued from the day before – enabling children to link into ideas over a longer period and develop them further. The play had originated from the stories and activities earlier on in the week about the three little pigs and keeping safe from the wolf. The learning story (narrative) shows how the idea had grown and the avenues it had taken, not just for one child but for a whole group.

The learning that was occurring related to children's language development through their imaginative talk, expressing ideas and negotiating with each other. There was clear evidence of mathematical development as the children worked out how many children they could pull up the slide, the amount of bricks that could fit into the bucket and building the door (fitting bricks together, selecting the number of bricks, checking the height and width) all problem solving and reasoning skills. The co-operation and collaboration of the children showed their developing personal, social and emotional skills through sharing, playing together and helping each other; physical development was clearly evident as children pushed and pulled, held onto the rope deciding how much energy to exert as well as climbing and balancing; knowledge of the world and expressive arts and design were noticeable through reinvention of ideas, the use of imagination and the scientific skills of force, balance and weight.

Adult support

The role of the adult in supporting children to make links and connections in their creative and critical thinking, learning and play has been woven throughout this chapter and throughout the book. Looking back on some of the observational case studies we can take a closer look at how the adults have supported and developed the children's creative and critical thinking.

Pause for thought

As we 'untangle' what we have seen in this case study it tells us a great deal about this group of children and what they are learning, particularly if we think about the areas of development communication and language, personal, social and emotional development, physical development, mathematical development, expressive arts and design and knowledge of the world. The narrative also tells us a great deal about how children are learning including their creative and critical thinking. The whole creation of the play is creative as this is the children's interpretation of their ideas.

Have a look at the indicators for creative thinking in Chapter 2 and see if you can recognise any of these in the children's play.

Links to practice

Observe a group of children playing together in your setting or school. Outdoor play is usually a great opportunity to do this as children become involved together. Take a sequence of photographs of the children as well as identifying children like Ammar who are busy on their own 'activity' within the group. Then untangle what you have seen thinking about **how** the children are learning as well as **what** they are learning.

Planning for the next steps or possibilities will need to focus on individual children, as well as the group, since the children will be at various points and will require different avenues of support and experiences.

How could you display this learning story so that everyone, including the children and their parents, can see what has happened and what might happen next?

The climbing frame

The adults at this nursery school and children's centre in Sheffield, supported the children's creative and critical thinking in these ways:

- Reading and telling stories about the three little pigs as well as other traditional stories. They had provided opportunities to talk about and discuss the stories together, with the children, and various ideas had arisen and were included in further planning/opportunities both indoors and outdoors.

- Children's ideas were listened to, acknowledged and recorded as they were followed up by the adults.

- All the adults were aware of what the children had said and how they were taking the ideas forward so that they could be supported as the children played in this large setting.

- Adults had provided materials and further provocations to extend children's ideas and encourage more talking and thinking e.g. they had set up the yellow bucket on a rope-pulley on the climbing frame.

- The adult observed the children as they played and intervened sensitively adding comments, thoughts and modelling ways to do things. She didn't do it for them, limit their actions or stop the rope pulling – she was there making sure that children were safe but having-a-go and helping each other; providing suggestions, helpful comments and enjoying the children's experiences. She made sure that the play developed and ideas were able to flow in what was quite a busy area, for example gradually the rope-pulling

moves around to the other side of the climbing frame and involved pulling children not the bucket.

- The same adult stayed with the play and followed it through, enjoying being outside and becoming completely involved in the play with the children but not imposing her own ideas. She was observing the children, storing it to memory to be later recalled with the team so that she could alert them to children's on-going progress and integrated into planning the next steps.

- Next steps or possibilities were planned for the next day and following week by adding new materials to the continuous provision e.g. ropes and pulleys were placed in other areas of outdoor play, tarpaulins and clips were added, a blanket on the nearby grass had non-fiction books about cranes, lifting and pulling machines and diggers as well as some clip boards, pencils and paper. The cameras were available for the children and adults to use.

- The learning story was read back to the children, after it had had been printed, so that they could reflect on their thinking and contribute further ideas. The adults also used this as an opportunity to clarify what the children had talked about as it was difficult to record all the conversation at the time. The story was then placed in the book area after being used outside to develop the play. It also formed part of a display on the children's ideas and thinking which was added over the following weeks.

Leo's story

The adults at this nursery school and children's centre in Sheffield, had supported Leo's creative and critical thinking by:

- Creating a calm, welcoming and stimulating environment for the children with many links to home. There were a good selection of open-ended materials, all of a high quality including water, sand play and dough.

- Supporting Leo as he was settling in so that he was confident and happy. The adults knew him well and had made firm, supportive relationships with Leo and his parents. Leo felt able to explore and follow his ideas.

- Knowing what Leo was interested in – pushing and transporting wheeled toys as well as being interested in lines (trajectories). They made sure that there were opportunities for him to do this indoors and outdoors.

- Observing Leo playing with the wheeled truck and recording the sequence of his play as it led from one thought to another. They could see how involved he was in the idea of wheeling two cars together and cleared a space so that he could do this safely and develop his balance and coordination. They used the observation to plan for his next steps and future possibilities (see Leo's Learning Story).

- Sharing his adventures and explorations with his mum and dad, showing them the photographs and the learning story and asking if they would like to add anything to the learning story and giving them a copy.

Playing with leeks

The adults at this Community Nursery and Children's Centre in Sheffield supported and developed Aakifah and Daniela's creative and critical thinking by:

- Being aware of the potential of this activity for stimulating children's curiosity and inquisitiveness. Not only did the activity support the development of children's finer manipulative skills and the smells, taste and texture of the vegetables it provided an opportunity to explore, experiment and look more closely at the properties of carrots and leeks.

- Participating in the activity alongside the children, modelling how to cut safely with a knife, teaching important skills, talking about the vegetables and developing the children's sense of smell, taste, touch. There was a 'homely' feel about the way the activity had been presented and shared together.

- Watching the children and following their lead as they peeled away the rings of the leek and looked at the strips, then poking their small fingers into the middle to see what would happen.

- Sharing in the children' excitement as the leek changed shape and covered their fingers; accepting their idea and modelling it with other interested children.

- Planning the next steps or possibilities by following the children's ideas and interests (see playing with leeks for further possibilities).

- By printing out the learning story and turning it into a 'book', reading it with the children and encouraging them to talk further about what they did and reflect on their thinking.

Emily and the frost

The conversation between Emily and her teacher Kath shows how the adult can support the development of sustained shared thinking through a conversation about the frost and by:

- Seeing an opportunity to provoke Emily's thinking and creativity and pointing out the frost on the grass. In this case Kath has 'batted a ball' to Emily (remember Malaguzzi's table tennis metaphor for co-constructing thinking).

- Waiting for a response from Emily and then building on what she said by using thoughtful questions, rather than closed or meaningless questions like 'what colour is it?'. The questions Kath uses have many more creative possibilities and will provoke critical thinking e.g. 'I wonder why that is?' and 'what do you mean?'.

- Being excited and involved in the exploration alongside Emily, responding to her ideas and thinking and building the learning together – keeping the ball in play!

- Keeping the conversation natural, shared and interesting; following its path together as partners (sensitive partner) and playing with ideas.

Chapter 3: Children make links

Pause for thought

The examples from the observations and learning stories show how complex and wide ranging the role of the adult is in supporting and extending children's creative and critical thinking. At times we do many of these things spontaneously in response to the children – especially when we know them well and have a great deal of experience. However, we do need to be aware of the complexities of the role and use these critical skills to support the development of babies, toddlers and young children.

> *"..the decision to encourage or limit creativity is related to the attitudes of the significant people who shape children's environments – whether they value creativity and are tolerant of the children's ideas… even if these may challenge their own viewpoints."*
> (Wright, p.4, 2010)

Links to practice

Think about your own practice and the way you use your knowledge and skills to support the children you are with.

Are you playing alongside children and modelling language, skills and actions? Do you become involved with the children and show interest in their ideas and excitement as you follow them through together? Are you a 'sensitive partner'?

It is important to stand back and reflect on your practice in order to develop and improve your knowledge and skills as a practitioner. Using a video camera can really help with this, as well as talking through what you are doing with a supportive mentor or asking a colleague to observe you in practice with the children.

- Maintaining a balance between adult-led learning (**K:** Have you seen the grass just here? Pointing to a frosty patch) and child-initiated learning (**E:** Because the frost isn't coming down there).

Enabling environment

If children are to make links and connections in their creative thinking and learning they need to see this represented in the environment around them. What we provide and the way we provide it should communicate a feeling of flexibility to connect ideas together, using different materials and tools which are readily available and not locked away. Good continuous provision meets this need very well so that children can be independent and are not always reliant on the adults. This also supports the development of self-regulation and means that the adult does not control everything; it is shared, supporting the balance between adult-led activities and child-initiated ideas and interests. For example, if a child has an idea and needs to use ribbons and tape they know where it is and can follow through their thinking straight away. Other ways of creating a flexible and connective environment include:

- Providing open-ended, imaginative material for babies (treasure baskets, cardboard boxes, coloured pieces of net, sand and water), toddlers (heuristic play, more cardboard boxes, guttering, builders trays, clay, fabric and pegs) and young children (more cardboard boxes, tarpaulins, drain piping, buckets, plastic pipes and tubes, large clumps of clay, large quantities of natural materials e.g. fir cones, conkers, pebbles, stones).

- Creating a flexible, imaginative environment which is not divided into overly structured, uninspiring areas which are labelled by the areas of learning e.g. maths area, literacy corner, writing area etc. The labelling of areas in this way immediately divide up and disconnect children's thinking and learning and in the process mean that some children will steer clear of the areas they are not interested in. For example, many boys will avoid the writing area as they see it as a place where they have to sit still and complete work (or worse worksheets) when, if they have access to clip boards or large chunks of chalk outside, they will happily engage in writing.

- Remembering that creating and thinking critically involves everything and not just creative activities or Expressive arts and design (DfE, 2012). For example, making Christmas,

Diwali or Eid cards which are all the same, using pre-cut outlines and glitter are not creative and do not involve a great deal of thinking by the children. No real connections are made or ideas followed and at worst, children have little or no understanding of the deeper meaning of these festivals and cultures. However if the children were able to decide how (and if) they wanted to represent Christmas, Diwali or Eid there should be many different interpretations, using all kinds of materials with various, diverse and unique ideas.

- Ensuring that children have the space, time and opportunity to play imaginatively with the freedom to combine resources, revisit ideas from the past and repeat playful experiences. Providing open-ended role play areas both indoors and outdoors; for example pop-up tents, deck chairs and pretend camp fires outside, dragons dens, creepy castles and secret dens made with recently trimmed tree branches or large cardboard boxes which have been joined together to create tunnels for toddlers to crawl through.

- Involving the children in the planning and asking them what they want to do next – tomorrow or next week and making sure that the play can be extended over a period of days and weeks.

Language and communication

Talking together and doing your thinking 'out loud' is fundamental to shaping your ideas and connecting them to other bits and pieces that you already know. It is even better when you can do this with others as sharing thinking through discussion really does help you to make the links; suddenly the 'light goes on' and you can see when a child has truly understood something quite significant. We can see this happening in the conversation between Emily and her teacher, Kath. Talking clarifies thinking and can lead to the generation of even more ideas which in itself is creative and will develop into the kind of lifelong learning skills that all children need to have in the future. The more opportunities children have to communicate and articulate their ideas and thinking, the more competent they become at 'making connections, being imaginative and creative and represent their experiences, ideas and relationships' (Bruce, p.10, 2004). We can see the way language and communication have supported children's creative and critical thinking in the observations and learning stories in Chapter 3, for example:

- Playing with language and making it fun as the children and adult did with the *Pat the Cat* story and making up rhymes

- Leo communicated through his actions and facial expressions but this needs to be extended into talk by the adult modelling language e.g. 'you are going fast Leo'.

- Using language in different ways like songs and rhymes

- Sharing the conversation and following the child's lead, balancing out adult-directed/led with child-initiated/led talk ; avoiding taking over with too many questions or sticking to your own agenda when the child has clearly lost interest.

Key points

This chapter has focused on how children make the links and connections in their thinking and learning and why that is so important. The main points to think about are:

- Children are already good connectors as they play, develop and learn in a holistic way which is woven and tangled together

- Children need many opportunities to connect their ideas and thinking so that it makes sense to them; rather like a huge jigsaw puzzle with thousands of pieces

- Children's early connections can be seen in their schematic play

- Sustained shared thinking is about children making links and connections as they interact and play with others, especially adults

- Narrative observations, which tell the whole story of children's developing ideas and thinking, help us to see the connections that they are making in their learning

- An environment which supports connections will be flexible, imaginative and open-ended with un-interrupted time to extend creative thinking both indoors and outdoors

- Talking together and sharing conversations is one of the best ways to connect ideas and develop thinking – as you talk together, creative and critical thinking grows.

Chapter 4: Children choosing ways to do things

All children are unique and will think, develop and learn in their own individual style. As a result they will find many different ways to do things as they explore the world around them. It is this uniqueness that makes babies, toddlers and young children creative in their own right, with an inner drive to interpret, understand and know the people, places and things around them. This is also one of the joys of being with young children – you never quite know what they are going to do or say next!

However, it also means that we need to be open and alert to the ways that babies, toddlers and young children choose

to do things since it can tell us a great deal about who they are, what they are thinking and how they are learning.

The following chapter will look in depth at this, including the following questions:

● How can adults (practitioners, teachers, parents) support children to choose ways to do things?

● How does the enabling environment support children to choose ways to do things?

Children choosing ways to do things

There is widespread recognition that babies, toddlers and young children *'develop and learn in different ways and at different rates'* (DfE, p.3, 2012); which means that children's development does not follow a neat, tidy pathway, with orderly steps to be achieved before progressing onto the next. The reality is that children's development is complicated, messy and tangled – it's the spaghetti model again. For example, some babies and toddlers will crawl and walk before they are a year old, whilst others will take longer, but their language development may have progressed further. Every child is different and much will depend on the experiences and support they receive from their parents, families and settings as to how they will tackle the many challenges ahead of them.

Crucially, as we nurture the ways in which children choose to do things, we are also nurturing them as independent, creative thinkers with ideas and views of their own, so that they can be independent and not reliant on others to do their thinking for them. It is these skills that contribute to children being in control of their learning, developing a positive mindset and becoming a self-regulated thinker and learner.

Children need to be able to develop their own ideas and 'point of view' (Bruce 2004) and try different ways of doing things in order to have something to be creative and think critically about; as a result they *'come to new and better understandings and ways of doing things'* (EYFS, 2008 Learning and Development Card 4.3). If we do everything for them or over-plan experiences we take away this autonomy and disempower children so that they become overly reliant on the adults to tell them what to do and how to do it.

Being able to choose the way to do something means that we need to trust children's instincts, their innate behaviours and their originality and allow them to have a go. Babies' although reliant on parents and carers for their basic needs will have some control over the situation through their early communication, for example, differing cries alert us to differing needs: 'I am hungry', or 'I am bored', or 'I am tired'. As they grow, they use other strategies to draw you into their play, for example by giving you the toy and then taking it back in a game of 'to and fro'.

Following patterns of thinking or schema will mean that children decide on their own way of doing something just as

Leo did with the push along cars. Becoming fascinated with something and taking an interest will lead to children deciding on strategies to use as they explore and experiment, as we saw with Blake and his ideas about water.

The learning story on pages 60-62 illustrates how Jalilah chose different ways to do things and how this influenced other children's ideas and thinking (look at this first before reading on).

What did we see?

This all began with a piece of wool which caught the interest of Jalilah and Scarlett. They were both fascinated by attaching the wool and then the string. I thought they would use the ball of string to wrap around the climbing bridge, but Jalilah had other ideas and decided to use shorter lengths of string.

The focus for Shanice, Malaikah and Ibrahim was on winding and tying, whilst Vivian and Omar wanted to trail it along behind the pram. They all took a piece of string and found different ways of using it – different ideas. There was string tied to the crates, the fence and the climbing bridge.

The play was mainly individual with children involved and concentrating on the wrapping and tying with their own piece of string. Gradually more children followed Jalilah's initial idea and the string play grew out of that.

Further possibilities?

Both Jalilah and Scarlett were involved and concentrating for the longest time on tying the string.

We could build on this by:

● Providing more materials to wrap and tie with e.g. rope, coloured tape, ribbon etc.

● Introduce weaving on a small and large scale both outdoors and indoors – could use the fences outside

● Show the string story to the children and ask them to comment on what they were doing and thinking about – add this to the learning story

● Share pictures with the children of Art in Nature – Andy Goldsworthy's work and art installations with string (Google).

CASE STUDY – playing with string

Jalilah and Scarlett were sat in the boxes together joined by a short piece of wool. They were trying to tie the boxes together and join them. Scarlett had wound it round her legs and Jalilah was looking for a way to join it to herself. They were very focused on the task watching each other and offering 'advice' on how to do it.

A little later the idea changed and they tied the wool to the climbing bridge, stretching it from one pole to the other. Shanice and Ibrahim came to help as well. They wanted to stretch the wool so that they could wrap it around but it wouldn't reach. Jalilah held on to the end and shouted to the others that there wasn't enough to go any further. I was standing nearby watching what was happening and went to find some more wool or string.

I gave the ball of string to Jalilah thinking that she would use it to wind around the climbing bridge as the children had with the string. But Jalilah said she wanted to cut a piece off and went to fetch the scissors.

She unwound a long piece of string and cut it – it was hard at first and she asked if I could do it. I said I would hold the string tight and that would make it easier to cut. Jalilah kept coming back for string and cutting it in the same way.

Choosing or deciding on the way to do something is directly connected to children initiating their own ideas and child-led play.

She took each piece of string and began to tie it to the post of the climbing bridge making sure that it didn't get tangled and straightening it out before wrapping it around.

With great care Jalilah passed the string around the post and tried to secure it by making a knot – it took several goes, a lot of persistence and careful wrapping with her fingers. She was really concentrating.

She pulled out the remaining string and checked that the knot was firm. I thought she would wrap the spare string around the climbing bridge but Jalilah was more interested in holding on to the end of the string and pulling it tight, then going back for another piece.

Several children were watching what Jalilah was doing and began to find ways of their own to tie the string. Malaikah decided to wrap her piece of string around herself. She wanted everyone to look.

CASE STUDY CONTINUED – playing with string

Ibrahim had been watching from a distance and then went to fetch his own piece of string, which he wrapped around the post and held on to, to stop it from unravelling.

Shanice had been involved in the wool wrapping and was keen to have her own piece of string wrapping it with great care around another post and concentrated on tying the end so that it was knotted. Shanice went on to do even more tying, threading and weaving with the pieces of string.

Vivian pulled the piece of wool along as Omar pushed the pram – they went all around the yard with the wool streaming behind.

> " Being able to choose the way to do something means that we need to trust children's instincts, their innate behaviours and their originality and allow them to have a go. "

What does this learning story tell us about the ways in which children choose to do things?

- Jalilah and Scarlett had already decided to sit in the boxes and play with the string – they were leading the play, it was their idea, they co-constructed it together

- Independently they both decided to extend this further by wrapping the wool around the climbing bridge and tying it

- They decided to work on this idea together, developing it through talking together, testing it out in other areas apart from the cardboard boxes

- With the arrival of the string, Jalilah decided that she needed shorter pieces and went to fetch the scissors, she then developed the idea into wrapping and tying which she spent a long time on

- The other children were interested in what was happening with the string and all made a decision to get their own piece, wrapping, tying and pulling it in their own unique way

- A little later on Shanice went on to weave the string in and out of the bread crates.

Self-regulation

Choosing or deciding on the way to do something is directly connected to children initiating their own ideas and child-led play. All children need to have this independence and autonomy in order to create the situations from which to make their own decisions and choices. Being able to choose from a limited range of adult-planned and structured activities reduces the choices and decisions that children can make, especially if they are uninspiring with little opportunity for imaginative and creative thinking. This is why good continuous provision is so important as it supports children's autonomy and allows them to make choices and decisions all of which contribute to them becoming creative and critical thinkers and learners.

The theoretical term for this autonomous, decision-making process is 'self-regulation' which has been referred to in the previous chapters. Ultimately as children become more able to make their own choices and decisions they will learn how to organise their own learning and plan their own next steps, which is all linked

Pause for thought

The children led the way on the string play, it was their idea and they chose how to start it and develop it. They had the opportunity, time and materials to do this with supportive adults observing their idea and then helping by fetching the string.

The adult then let the children decide what to do with the string, which was not what she had originally expected they would do. As a result, the string play went on for most of the afternoon and extended into the days and weeks afterwards. It also drew in other children who made their own creative decisions about how to use the string. It seems that choosing ways to do things involves a great deal of decision-making individually and collaboratively, which is a substantial part of being able to think critically.

Links to practice

How do you provide opportunities and materials to enable children to make their own decisions?

As you observe your children, can you see the ways in which they are choosing to do something? What does this look like? Take some photographs and note down when this is happening and share it with the other adults – you could even display the pictures and show the children, parents and other adults just how children make their choices.

to having the interest, motivation and desire to carry on wanting to find out more, wanting to be a learner and becoming an independent, imaginative thinker. These are the kind of lifelong-learning attitudes, dispositions and skills that we want for all children and should definitely be included in their internal 'tool kit'.

Self-regulation actually has its roots at birth in good early attachment and attunement, where the baby's needs are all met (regulated) by the parents/carers. As the baby grows and starts to walk and talk they are moving towards more independence from the parent/carer but still require the loving, nurturing support they give.

Chapter 4: Children choosing ways to do things

Gradually the child will be able to regulate some of his/her own needs like going to the toilet, asking for a cuddle, wanting a story or asking a question. With consistent love and support, as well as the right opportunities, the child will become more confident and motivated to become engaged in play and activities, finding out and exploring, seeking out challenges and persisting at what they are doing. They will know that it is okay if it doesn't work out or goes wrong and find other ways to do things. It is through their play that children really become self-regulated thinkers and see themselves as successful, capable and competent learners.

'As self-regulated thinkers and learners children will be able to plan their next steps and organise their own outcomes. In short, they take responsibility for their own learning' (Chilvers, D., p.4, 2012).

Pause for thought

The children's charter for thinking and learning takes the perspective of the children and how they learn best. Each point is based on what the practitioners saw the children doing as they followed their own ideas and interests. It was important to acknowledge the children's voices and recognise how competent and capable they were as thinkers and learners – with supportive adults around them who observed their developing ideas, helped them to make links and provided them with opportunities and time to decide on ways to do things and try them out.

Links to practice

The children's charter for thinking and learning encompasses all the three characteristics – playing and exploration, active learning and creating and thinking critically. Looking back at the characteristics grid, in the introduction to this book, think about how the children's voices in the charter link to all these aspects. It's a good idea to talk together about this with others as it helps to reflect on your own philosophy and practice.

A small practitioner research study at a children's centre in Sheffield in 2007 followed the decisions and choices of a group of three and four-year-olds by following their ideas and interests. We observed the children's learning journey's noting down the things they said and did, the choices and decisions they made as well as their excitement and eagerness to follow their interests in cars, trains, music and messy materials.

As we followed the children and listened to their voices it became clear to us that there were certain things they needed to do and be, in order to follow their ideas, make links and connections and choose ways to do things. We called it 'The children's charter for thinking and learning'.

The children's charter for thinking and learning

- I make sense of my world in my own unique way through what interests me.

- I view myself as a competent thinker and learner.

- I am a different kind of thinker from an adult – what interests me is very different from what interests adults.

- I like to construct my learning together with the other children and adults around me.

- When I follow my interests I begin to think in a much 'deeper way'. I can 'unpick' my ideas and 'explore' through the activities I am interested in.

- I spend a long time at the activities that interest me. I concentrate for longer, become very involved and persist at what I am doing.

- When I am interested in an activity I want to keep coming back to it day after day. I get excited about my learning, it's fun and I enjoy it – I want to do more.

- I like my thinking and learning to be real and to be part of something interesting, like trains, messy play, people and music. I don't want my learning to be separated into pieces like literacy, numeracy, geography – I learn in a holistic way.

- When I can follow my interests and adults support me (and are interested as well), this makes me feel good. Then I feel

Children choosing ways to do things in the case studies

Children choosing ways to do things…		
Babies	Toddlers	Young children
Jessica is…	Leo is…	The children on the climbing frame playing with the bricks are.
• making a **conscious decision** about what she wants to look at in the treasure basket • choosing to **explore** the materials by **looking** inside them, **feeling** them, **banging** them together, looking at them closely • choosing to **concentrate** really hard and focus on the interesting objects – she is **not distracted** • choosing which objects to play with for longer than the others and which ones she wants to know more about by '**talking** with' granny	• making a **conscious choice** to play with the wheeled truck/s and has **remembered** this from the day before • choosing to **test out** his ideas further and **refine** them by finding another truck • **building his hypothesis** about balancing the trucks together and synchronising how he pushes them • **solving any problems** he encounters by **repeating** and **practicing** • choosing to **share his ideas** with his friend who comes along and wants to have a go	• choosing to **play together** and **individually** with the pulley and the bricks • **sharing** their ideas and **collaborating** as the play progresses – helping each other and making suggestions • Diana has chosen to be the 'supplier' of the bricks – she has **taken on a role**. Whilst Ammar has chosen to be the builder and build the door • **exploring** different ways to pull the bucket of bricks and the other children up the slide • **listening** to the adult when she offers help and support • **involved** and **concentrating** as they play – **talking** to each other and **sharing** their thinking • **solving their own problems** and thinking of **other possibilities** like using the rope in different ways
The words that are highlighted are some of the main strategies that children choose to use in order to find out more about their worlds. We need to look out for these strategies and take note of them in our observations as they will tell us a great deal about children's creative and critical thinking.		

confident, secure and happy. I trust people and make good relationships with them.

• When I follow my interests, my 'thinking language' becomes more creative. I will invent words like 'clunks' and 'bobbles' to explain what I mean and be very creative. I like to think out loud and I can do this through my talk. I can also do this through my non-verbal expressions, through my behaviour, through watching others and through my drawings, pictures and models. You just have to listen to me.

• When I follow my interests I can offer my own ideas and express them. I can build them up with other children and

adults. I can sustain my thinking and share it with those around me.

Observing babies, toddlers and young children

Babies, toddlers and young children will use a whole range of strategies to enable them to make choices and decisions about how to do something. We can gain an insight into these quite complex skills through watching children as they are engaged in their play, but we need to know what we are looking for so that we can recognise the creative nature of their critical thinking.

Chapter 4: Children choosing ways to do things

If we are to say that a child is a critical thinker we need to know what that looks like. The following are some of the main things to consider and look for in your observations.

Play

Undoubtedly, the most significant strategy that babies, toddlers and young children use to find out, explore and make decisions and choices, is play. All children, including babies and toddlers have a natural desire to engage in play as one of the main ways they can find out about themselves and their environment: it is how they make sense of the world they are in, how they grow their ideas and try them out and how they connect their experiences together. Indeed, play is a creative activity in itself as this is the place where children's ideas and imagination can flow. The children's stories in this book are confirmation of this, showing the many opportunities for creative and critical thinking.

If you reflect back on the learning stories and the children's play, we can see the many ways that they are choosing to do things and making decisions. The table on page 65 highlights some of the ways babies, toddlers and young children choose to do things.

Babies, toddlers and young children will use play as a way of gathering the information they need about the people, places and things around them (hoovering up experiences), they will come to understand how things work and what they can do with them.

Increasingly, as children become more confident and skilful, they will widen their ideas and interests and share them with others. It is at this point that play takes on a new perspective in that it has a focus and drive which comes from the children; it has been initiated by them and has grown out of their interests and ideas; it has a creative flow which generates 'flexible thinking' (Whitebread, 2012). Adults need to tune-in to this play and support the development of the children's ideas by becoming involved and extending creative and critical thinking further – otherwise the play may become tired and aimless.

Imaginative play has a substantial purpose in creative and critical thinking, offering many opportunities for children's ideas to flow and for using different strategies to find out and explore. For example, the creative act of role-play enables children from a very young age to transfer their thinking from their own view point or perspective to another. Being able to choose imaginative strategies like pretend play (I am on the moon, I am in an aeroplane), being someone or something else (the mummy/daddy, the cat, the monster, spider man), or being in another place (the bear's house, the moon, a castle) all contribute to their developing view of the world and involve wonderful moments of creative thinking as well as creative language.

Vivien Gussin-Paley's work over many years has been a strong voice for children's creative and imaginative play, with the recognition of wonderfully constructed stories from the ideas that children constructed in their play. Here is a typical example:

> *"Peter Rabbit is a robber, you know," says five-year-old William, as Theresa, age four, pours two cups of tea. "But I don't think I drink tea if I am a robber."*
>
> *Theresa pushes a cup closer to William. "You could have it because it's chamillia-willia tea. That means it's for you because you're a William."*
>
> *"But I'm a robber. They don't drink tea"*
>
> *"Peter is not a robber. Oh no"*
>
> *"He steals the lettuce, so he is a robber"*
>
> *"Mr McGregor is mean. So it's okay for Peter to do that. And I'm your mother. You can't be a robber if I'm waiting for you"* (Gussin-Paley, p.58, 2004).

Some of the strategies children use when they are creating and thinking critically

Strategies that children choose...	What does this mean?	What does this look like?
Problem setting and problem solving	Setting and solving problems means that you have to think creatively and critically in order to work them out and reach a possible solution. It is the process of solving the problem that requires the critical thinking and creativeness – you have to be able to think out of the 'box'. It will involve trial and error, experimenting, repeating and practicing – so look out for this when you are observing. Conversational talk will be a big part of problem setting and problem solving as children become more able to articulate their thinking and solutions – their ideas to solve the problem will be highly creative and imaginative.	We can see and hear the many ways that children solve problems in the case studies and the examples of Emily in the frost and the children sorting out what good and bad mean. You could present the children with a problem and see what happens – for example – a letter arrives from Goldilocks saying she is unable to make contact with the bears to apologise for eating the porridge and breaking the chair. What should she do? For babies and toddlers problem setting is more about physical action like 'how do I make the water wheel go around' or 'how can I envelop myself in the blanket'.
Reasoning	An important process in being able to think creatively and critically – which requires children being able to explore their ideas, hypothesise – make theories e.g. 'I think it's because...', ask questions, and puzzle out. It includes recognising when things are not working or are not right – getting it wrong and trying again – working it out e.g. 'what do I do with this, how does it work?'. Being able to predict what might happen next or explain something all require reasoning	Look out for children, babies and toddlers being curious (like Jessica, Leo, Aakifah, Daniela and Natalia), puzzling out how things work – taking them apart and trying to put them back together, what they feel like, what happens when they push or pull or bang something. For babies and toddlers reasoning is more about finding out the information about something – what is it, what does it taste, sound like, feel like etc. As children get older they are able to think 'if I can do this with this then I can change it to this...'.
Possibility thinking	Is about children finding and solving problems by themselves and with each other – 'it lies at the heart of the creative process' (DCSF, 2010) and involves using the imagination and leads to critical thinking. It involves the use of possibility questions by both the children and the adults to construct and sustain thinking. Possibility questions might include: What does that remind you of? What do you think might happen next? Is there another way...? What do you think? How could you/we do that?	Babies will be exploring and finding out about materials and objects – what is it? What does it do? They are information gathering which will support later ideas about the possibilities of the materials. E.g. Jessica and Leo. Toddlers will build on this new found 'information' and start to explore the possibilities of what they can do with the materials so developing their early ideas e.g. Leo, Aakifah and Daniela. Young children will be developing even more imaginative and interesting possibilities with the materials around them e.g. playing with the crates and string. They will be very absorbed and involved in what they are doing either independently or collaboratively – the possibilities will be the ideas and interests the children create and follow.

Chapter 4: Children choosing ways to do things

Some of the strategies children use when they are creating and thinking critically

Strategies that children choose…	What does this mean?	What does this look like?
Metacognition	May sound complicated but is actually a built-in part of good early years practice. It is when we encourage children to think and reflect on their thinking so thinking about your thinking. It includes being able to use a range of strategies – including the ones listed here – and deciding what to do, how to do it and following a train of thought. Then, as they become even more aware of their thinking, being able to recount what they did and explain how it worked. 'It is how children become aware of themselves as thinkers and how they reflect on their thinking, but in order to do this they have to have their thinking and ideas acknowledged by the people around them' (Chilvers, p.24, 2012).	You can, at times, almost see the cogs turning as you watch babies, toddlers and young children by looking at their facial expressions, eyes and furrowed brows. There is clearly some thinking going on which we need to be aware of and acknowledge. So look for this as you observe. You can see it in Jessica's facial expression. Look for children exploring, trying things out and problem setting/solving, it will also be evident as they reason and think things through. Repeating something will be a sign of children re-visiting their thinking either on their own or with others. Look for children playing together and co-constructing their ideas – also with adults.
Talking, discussing and having conversations	Communication, language, talk and conversation are one of the key strategies that children choose to use to make their thinking known. Cognitive development (thinking, reasoning, problem solving, metacognition) and language development are inextricably linked – they both support the development of each other. Conversational talk is particularly important as this is where a lot of thinking is constructed.	Babies' communication can be recognised through their cries, cooing, tongue and lip movements, facial expressions and body movements. Their earliest conversations are face to face with their family as they 'talk' with each other and take turns. Young children's language will be increasing rapidly and as long as they are encouraged and acknowledged, their imaginative, thinking language will increase. It's important to record what children are saying as this tells us a great deal about their thinking.
Asking questions	Chapter 1 considered the fundamental need for children to ask their own questions as they develop their creative and critical thinking. Questions are windows into children's worlds and thinking so we need to listen to their enquiries and thoughts. They are also central to problem solving, reasoning and sustained shared thinking – it's difficult to use any of these strategies if you don't ask questions – but they need to come from the children with adults using a minimum and making sure they are reflective, thought provoking questions that extend thinking. The use of possibility questions by adults and children are very important as using these type of open-ended, searching and reflective questions will help children to compose similar ones.	Babies will ask questions in their own way by looking at you, eye contact, facial expressions, crying, cooing etc. It's important that adults respond to this by talking to the baby, as this provokes a conversation. Toddlers' questions become more refined, they may use a pointed finger and a sound which gradually turns into a word e.g. 'what's that?'. They may take your hand and show you, or pull your face that way. Older children's questions will be more refined and usually include a lot of 'why' questions. They may need you to help them frame their questions e.g. 'Oh I see you want to know why…'. The use of possibility questions by adults is very important as this will help children to compose similar ones.

Pause for thought

There are many other strategies that children will use to do things, which is why it is important to observe the whole process of their thinking rather than just a snapshot. Otherwise, we may miss a critical moment when the child suddenly comes to understand or creates a truly imaginative solution to a problem. Encouraging children to look back at the observation with you, and sharing the photographs or what you have written will enable them to explain what they did (metacognition) and add to the story of the observation.

Links to practice

Share an observation with the children, show them the pictures and/or tell them the story of what you saw them do and say, discuss it together and see how this develops their ideas, interests and thinking even further. Don't forget to record what the children say.

The children's imaginative play is recognised by Gussin-Paley as *"a conversation of great merit. The logic is clear: robbers do not have mothers who wait for them and give them tea"* (p.58, 2004). As the children talk together in their different roles they have chosen to use the play to solve the problem of 'who is good' and 'who is bad' bouncing ideas off each other and looking for solutions as they think it through – this is creative and critical thinking in action.

When you are observing children playing and involved in creative and critical thinking these are some of the other strategies they will use. The table on pages 67 and 68 highlights some of the strategies children may use as they are involved in creative and critical thinking. Look out for these when you are observing the children.

Adult support

Although each of the chapters in this book have included the ways in which adults can support and extend children's creative and critical thinking, it is important to realise that these strategies can be used in many ways and in many situations: they are universal strategies, all part of good early years pedagogy and practice. So, the support for children having their own ideas and making links will be much the same for supporting children as they choose ways to do things.

Some other universal strategies that adults can use to support children as they choose ways to do things are:

- Acknowledge children's ideas and ways of doing things, avoid being prescriptive and overly directing children as they will become dependent on you for everything and will not try things for themselves or develop their own ideas. This will not support their positive mind-sets or the development of self-regulation habits.

- Make sure that you have a flexible, collaborative approach to child-initiated/led ideas and play with supportive and relevant adult-led activities.

- Listen to and talk with babies, toddlers and young children, taking what they say or communicate as your lead. Making sure that you do not dominate the conversation but are an equal partner, adding thoughts, comments and possibility questions as you construct the thinking together.

- Keeping your questions to a minimum and using them to develop children's ideas and thinking. If children are not sure what to do next or how to do something suggest some other strategies they could use and ask possibility questions such as 'have you thought about….. ?', ' I wonder if you could try…', 'If you did know what would you say…?'.

- Encourage children to retell how they did something e.g. 'why did you decide to do it that way?', 'was there another way to do it?'. Share your observation, especially the sequenced photographs with the children and ask them what they were doing and why, as well as pointing out when they look like they are puzzling over something or very involved, and ask 'what were you thinking here?'.

- Encourage the children to help each other and develop collaborative play and activities where they can share thinking and ways to do things, e.g. 'can you tell Connor how you did that as it might help with what he is doing?'.

- Add provocations to get the children thinking e.g. tell the children about your rescued cats and your concerns about

Chapter 4: Children choosing ways to do things

Play is the most effective way of ensuring that babies, toddlers and young children have the opportunities they need to be creative and critical thinkers.

An enabling environment

The continuing message throughout this chapter and the previous ones is that play is the most effective way of ensuring that babies, toddlers and young children have the opportunities they need to be creative and critical thinkers; having their own ideas, making links and choosing ways to do things. We need to exploit the natural power of play and children's innate magnetic need to partake of it and go with them on their imaginative, inquisitive and thoughtful quest to find out, think and learn. Play has just about everything that children need to be creative and critical thinkers:

how they are hiding because they are scared. Ask them what they think would be best for the cats – what should you do?

- Get involved in the babies, toddlers and young children's play – modelling strategies and ways to do things, playing alongside and mirroring what the children are doing, taking on a role and draw the children into the imaginative play and possibilities.

- Learn how to step back and wait, watching the children to see what is happening before you intervene or join in – think about your own strategies for doing things e.g. watcher/observer, supporter, modeller, play partner, sensitive companion, mediator, adviser, co-constructer, teacher…

- Make sure that children have the time, space and opportunity to problem-set and problem-solve so that they are able to explore, try things out and take safe risks. Let them return to things as they need to and keep them going for as long as possible.

- Above all celebrate the children's imaginative ideas and thinking, share it by displaying their pictures, photographs plans etc. on the wall, record it through your observations and share this back with the children especially in the form of learning stories, and make sure that parents and families are involved in the process.

'Children's play, crucially allows them to develop this 'flexibility' of thought because it allows them to try out different ways of looking at the world, different strategies to deal with problems and difficulties, and different ways of thinking, all within a safe context with no consequence' (Whitebread, D., p.64, 2012).

The following are some of the universal elements of an enabling environment, which supports children as they choose ways to do things:

- Continuous provision for babies, toddlers and young children, which is well laid out and presented, of a high quality and with many open ended materials and possibilities. Children will need to choose the tools and materials to develop their ideas and interests so they should be readily available. Adults need to be alert to when things should be added or enhanced to support developing ideas or provoke new ones.

- Indoor and outdoor experiences should be equal and consistent – with continuous provision available for use outside and in all weathers. Children's ideas, interests and thinking may take off when they are outside rather than inside, look at the examples in the learning stories, most of them are outside!

- Think about the materials and equipment you have and how many opportunities they hold for being used in different ways, and their imaginative and creative possibilities. Do you provide open-ended materials for role play, opportunities for children to decide on the role play and develop it themselves? E.g. blankets, pegs, poles, tarpaulins for den making, cardboard boxes on a large scale with tape, string, fabric etc.

- Are there materials to be creative with on a large and small scale inside and outside? E.g. paint, pastels, chalks, clay, dough, collage, glue, box modelling, woodwork, weaving, sewing, pattern making, music making, storymaking, dancing and singing…

- Observe what the children are doing with the materials and how they are using the spaces you have provided – is this telling you anything? Do you feel that the environment is enabling? Does it stimulate and encourage creative and critical thinking for all children? Can babies, toddlers and young children play imaginatively? Observation can tell you a great deal about the quality of your environment.

- Does the enabling environment encourage, communication, talking and conversation? Can children chatter together, exchange ideas and construct their thinking? Are children able to do their thinking out loud? Are there opportunities for children to record what they say?

Key points

This chapter has focused on how children choose ways to do things and why that is so important for the development of their creative and critical thinking. The main points to think about are:

- All children are unique and will think, develop and learn in their own individual style.

- Children's development does not follow a neat, tidy pathway, with orderly steps to be achieved before progressing onto the next.

- Choosing or deciding on the way to do something is directly connected to children initiating their own ideas and child-led play.

- Continuous provision is important as it supports children's autonomy and allows them to make choices and decisions all of which contribute to them becoming creative and critical thinkers and learners.

- As self-regulated thinkers and learners children will be able to plan their next steps and take responsibility for their own learning.

- The children's charter for thinking and learning.

- The universal strategies that adults can use to support children as they choose ways to do things.

- Play is the most effective way of ensuring that babies, toddlers and young children have the opportunities they need to be creative and critical thinkers, having their own ideas, making links and choosing ways to do things.

Chapter 5:
A thoughtful approach

The previous chapters have taken a close look at what it means to be a creative and critical thinker and the aspects which underpin this; children have their own ideas, make links across their ideas and find ways to make their ideas happen. This is not an easy process for the child or the adult, as it requires a thoughtful approach and good understanding of the ways in which babies, toddlers and young children develop and learn.

Susan Isaacs recognised this so many years ago and it is still very relevant today:

'*The child's world. It cannot, of course, be very easy for us to gain a clear idea of what the world is like to a very young child, just because it must be so different from our own. But by patient listening to the talk of even little children, and watching what they do, with the one purpose of understanding them, we can imaginatively feel their fears and angers, their bewilderments and triumphs; we can wish their wishes, see their pictures and think their thoughts*' (Isaacs, S., p.15, 1929).

This is the essence of the thoughtful approach adults need to take as they engage with young children in their world of creative and critical thinking. A thoughtful approach means standing back and asking some important questions about our practice, some of which have been included throughout the book in the 'Pause for thought' sections and links to practice, and other questions such as 'what did I just see?', 'why am I doing it this way and is it the best way for the child/children?''. These are the questions that make us think and reflect on our practice which in turn develop and improve the way we support children.

'A thoughtful approach' also means standing back and observing what the children are doing, saying and thinking and becoming aware of their ideas and interests. In Susan Isaacs's nursery school, The Malting House, observation was at the heart of everything, with richly documented dialogue, ideas and playful learning. Children's thinking, their proposals, hypotheses and ideas were all recorded and thoughtfully discussed by the adults who supported them, as this was the key way in which they learned about children and their development.

Key themes and messages

There are some key themes and messages about babies, toddlers and young children on Creating and thinking critically throughout the book, which require this thoughtful approach to improve and transform the quality of experiences in the early years. They include:

- The central role of observation and recording the children's thinking as it unfolds in a narrative or story

- The co-construction of thinking in collaborative ways including the importance of language, talk and conversation

- Recognising that babies, toddlers and young children have their own ideas and interests and letting them lead the learning

- Open-ended play as a place where all children do their most creative and imaginative thinking and talking

- The elements of being a critical and creative thinker such as possibility thinking, mindsets, self-regulation, problem setting and problem solving, reasoning and asking questions

- The 'tool kit' of skills and dispositions for being a creative and critical thinker which support children's learning for life and not just as a preparation for the next step

- Understanding that the way in which babies, toddlers and young children think, develop and learn is woven together in a tangle of spaghetti – it is holistic

- Adults being reflective and asking questions of their practice

- Providing imaginative materials for children to be creative with and to support critical thinking.

Transitions and future pathways for children

If adults support children's creative and critical thinking in this way, they will be ensuring that they become the motivated, thoughtful, imaginative learners of the future. However, this is not an easy path to take in a world where quick results and fast-tracking are increasingly seen as more acceptable. We have to be clear about what sort of a future we want for our children in a world that is constantly changing and becoming a global society; and what sort of creative and critical thinking will be required to survive in that future generation. Certainly where children and adults can think creatively, be self-regulated and solution-focused they will be adaptable, forward thinking and flexible to take on different types of work and activities.

However, before the future of life outside school, young children have to progress from the early years phase into their first years of schooling – where the transition from one setting to another should maintain the momentum of the child's early experiences and the confidence and well-being they hopefully bring with them. Transition is not just about making sure that children understand where they are moving to, who their new teacher

> **A thoughtful approach also means standing back and observing what the children are doing, saying and thinking and becoming aware of their ideas and interests.**

Chapter 5: A thoughtful approach

will be, who will be in their class, what the routines will be like and staying for school dinners. This is important and should be handled sensitively and with support by both the setting they are moving from and to and by their family. Much is written about the transition that the child has to make but little is said about the transition of philosophy and practice.

If we are to maintain the momentum and independence of young children as they move from an early years philosophy; that fosters creative and critical thinking, the flow of ideas and children's interests as well as the co-construction of learning, then they need to 'travel' into a similar philosophy which picks up from the previous one and builds on their thinking. Frequently this is where children's thinking and learning 'stalls' or even worse, regresses, as they experience an overly formal, adult-directed and timetabled curriculum which leaves no room for creativity and developing your own thinking. This is where a fixed mindset becomes the norm and children wait to be told what to do next. Children can no longer make their own choices, decide what to do next and follow their ideas and interests. In this case, there are many questions to be considered about transition, mainly around the school philosophy and environment being ready for young children to continue to become independent, creative thinkers and learners.

Some schools are already aware of the benefits of a curriculum that builds on the foundations of a good early years philosophy (described in this book and the others in the series). Many of these schools are following a curriculum that supports children's creativity and critical thinking, active learning and play and exploration and finding that children are continuing to be curious and independent thinkers and learners.

The following case study is from a school in Doncaster whose philosophy is based on starting from the children's creativity, interests and questions. We can see in the case study how the children's questions and interests shape what they do, as well as the way thinking and learning are woven together holistically, with adults supporting children's ideas as well as planning adult-led focused activities.

Did dragons exist?

The children in the reception class were interested in knights, castles and dragons, which the teachers picked up on and decided to ask a creative question: 'Did dragons exist?'.

The school follows a creative curriculum called Cornerstones, which is based on the original questions of children and supports the balance between child-initiated play and learning and adult-led focused activities and support.

If we look at this learning story of the children's involvement in finding out if dragons existed, what can we see in relation to their creative and critical thinking?

Having their own ideas

- The children's ideas have been picked up by the teachers and used to shape the curriculum and planning

- Children and teachers continue to share and bounce ideas between each other through talking, playing and activities

- The ideas have been used to plan next steps and inform the teaching

- The children have had the time to play with their ideas and develop them using a ranges of materials and working collaboratively and individually

- Materials have been widely available all of the time.

CASE STUDY – starting points

The interest developed with a question (something to think about): 'Did dragons exist?'. The provocation was given to the children (aged 5+) by their teachers as part of their creative curriculum, aiming to get children to talk together, think creatively, hypothesise and problem solve. What could be the possible answers to this question?

The play developed as the children became more interested in castles, knights and dragons. It included making imaginative stories using the small world castle and figures and building castles and lots of talk 'raise the draw bridge' using the wooden blocks. The children took on the parts of the characters they had created and gave directions and orders, "Pull up the drawbridge there's a dragon coming". They played collaboratively, concentrating for long periods of time and becoming very involved in the stories.

The teachers recorded what the children did and said using photographs and making notes and used this to plan the next steps.

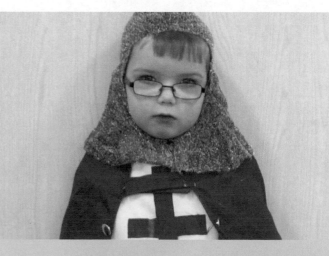

The teachers invited Sir Percival the Knight and his dragon to visit the class (the knight was a member of staff) to provoke more thinking and develop the children's ideas about knights, castles and dragons. They told the story of the knight and his dragon and spoke with the children.

The conversation between them and the children developed with the children asking lots of questions. This led to even more ideas, inspiring the children, who in the following days became engaged in role play, building a castle and finding clothes to wear as well as preparing a banquet.

CASE STUDY CONTINUED – starting points

The role play grew after the knight and dragon's visit – with children creating their own stories and becoming knights, princesses, kings and queens. They made the props they needed like the castle, swords, horses, banquet food and brought in dressing up outfits from home. The children recreated things from the stories they had heard, the discussions they had *with each other and the teachers and the significant moments that had been planned. The children's ideas were supported by the teachers giving them the time, space and opportunities to construct their thinking and follow their interest. Planning was based on observing the children as they were playing and involved in conversations.*

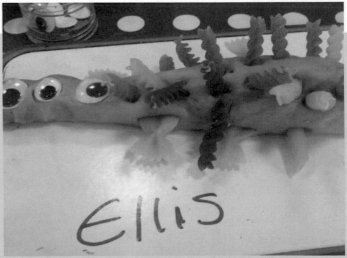

Some 'real' dragons came to school along with snakes and spiders and the children began to look more closely at other types of dragons. They found out about the lives, habits and make up of bearded dragons. They were able to touch them, hold them and take a very close look which led to much discussion both at the time and afterwards. *In the following days and weeks they recreated the experience through their drawing, painting, collage, clay, dough and writing.*

Making links

- The children's ideas about dragons have been extended by thinking about 'real' dragons and mystical ones. The visit by the knight and dragon puppet and the bearded dragons provoked the children's thinking and made connections to other aspects of their learning.

- Children have made the connection between their own ideas and how to create and represent them including through their writing.

- There has been plenty of discussion and talk to enable children to develop their ideas and make links with each other.

- The teachers have documented the children's 'stories'.

Choosing ways to do things

- The children have used a range of appropriate and meaningful ways to really think about what it means to be a dragon, e.g. role play, sword play, creating castles, taking a first-hand, close look at dragon like animals and deciding how to deal with a baby dragon.

- Experiences have included problem setting, problem solving and reasoning.

- Children have made their own decisions about what to do next and when. They are excited, eager and motivated to keep on trying and be involved.

- They are enjoying thinking and learning together and want to continue.

The children in this reception class became fully involved in the creative adventure of finding out if dragons did exist, so for them this was an experience of learning that had real meaning and intention. They could see the point of it and were motivated to keep on trying, become involved and concentrate for long periods and as a result they engaged in more talk and discussion, played collaboratively and cooperated with each other, read and shared books and poems and were more than happy to write. They were finding thinking and learning irresistible, which is what we would want all children to feel at every stage of their school experience.

Interestingly, the dispositions, skills and attitudes that have been a focus in this book and which shape the child's 'toolkit', are all transferable and can be used and developed throughout their lives. As learnacy skills they are equally important in the early years, primary and secondary school and as such can be built upon, refined and extended. They all support how children learn, rather than what children learn and need to build and develop seamlessly from one transition to the other.

Leading good practice

Leading good early years practice is the responsibility of everyone who works with young children. This aspiration springs from research over the past ten years, which shows that it is the quality of practitioners who will make the most difference to children's early development and learning (EPPE, 2004, REPEY, 2002, SPEEL, 2002) as long as they are rooted in understanding the development of babies, toddlers and young children and how they learn. Practitioners who are reflective and frequent observers of children will finely tune and refine their knowledge and experience to become experts at listening to and supporting children's development at a critical period in their lives. Reading this book, reflecting with others on the points in 'Pause for thought' and thinking about the links to practice, will be an effective foundation on which to build good practice.

A final thought

All practitioners, pedagogues, childminders and teachers play a critical role in young children's lives. However the most important adults for the child are their parents/carers, siblings and wider family. It is the child's parents and family who will have the biggest influence on their development, thinking and learning and the progress they make in their lives, which is why working in partnership together is so critical. The home learning environment does not need to be a replica of what happens in the setting, but it does need parents/carers who will listen and talk together with their children, support their ideas and interests through sharing conversations, looking at books together and supporting their child's play, enjoying the unfolding development of their child.

One of the most powerful ways we can share the joy of children's thinking and development is through observation and the type of learning stories described in this book. There is nothing more compelling than seeing how your child has thought something through and created an idea that was in their head. We can share this unfolding thinking, step by step, through photographs, film and audio tape.

CASE STUDY – finding the dragons egg

One morning the children found a dragon egg underneath a cushion where it was warm. The dragon egg was 'planted' to provoke the children's responses and language as well as getting them to think about how it got there. 'What do we do next? How do we look after the egg?'. It stirred their imagination and furthered discussion.

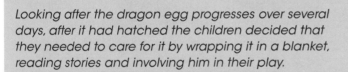

Looking after the dragon egg progresses over several days, after it had hatched the children decided that they needed to care for it by wrapping it in a blanket, reading stories and involving him in their play.

The adults supported all of their ideas and gave them the responsibility of what to do, when and how. The children shared their thoughts about the dragons care in a collaborative partnership, which included negotiation, planning and thinking ahead – they took this role very seriously.

The original question that had been posed by the teachers was: 'Did dragons exist?'. They offered the question to the children as a starting point for creative thinking, active learning and play and exploration and then supported the children's growing ideas and interest by following their lead and adding in memorable, planned moments

to extend their thinking and learning. The whole experience was co-constructed in partnership between the children and the teachers with a balance of child-initiated ideas and adult led/ focused activities resulting in some deep and meaningful thinking and learning. The children were inspired to write about their experiences.

> **They were finding thinking and learning irresistible, which is what we would want all children to feel at every stage of their school experience.**

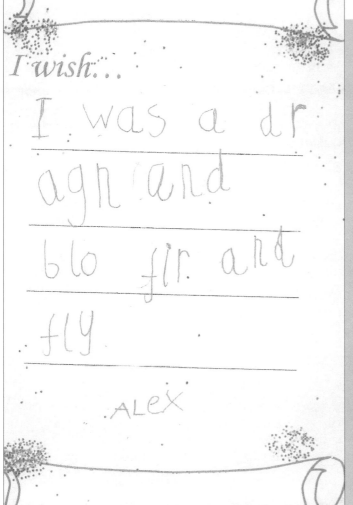

I wish…
I was a dr
agn and
bb flr ant
fly.

ALex

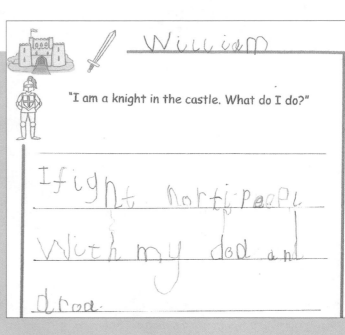

William

"I am a knight in the castle. What do I do?"

I fignt nortipeepl
with my dod ant
droa.

The children, boys and girls, were keen to write and saw this as a natural extension of their quest to find out if dragons existed.

The teachers has made sure that the writing tasks were embedded into realistic activities like invitations to the banquet, wishes and mystical stories as well as job descriptions of what a knight, princess, king, queen or dragon should do.

Writing happened anywhere and at any time.

References

Chapter 1

Bruce, T. (2004) *Cultivating Creativity in Babies, Toddlers and Young Children*, Hodder and Stoughton.

Chilvers, D. (2006) *Young children talking: The art of conversation and why children need to chatter*, Early Education.

Claxon, G. (2000) Transcript of a lecture 'A Sure Start for an uncertain world' *Early Education Journal* (Spring).

Craft, A. (2010) Teaching for Possibility Thinking. What is it and how do we do it? *Learning Matters*, Vol 15 Number 1.

DCSF (2008) Early Years Foundation Stage (www.education.gov.uk).

DfE (2012) Statutory Framework for the Early Years Foundation Stage (www.education.gov.uk).

Duffy (1998), *Supporting Creativity and Imagination in the Early Years*, Open University Press.

Edwards, C., Gandini, L., Forman, G. (1998) *The Hundred Languages of Children*, The Reggio Emilia Approach – Advanced Reflections, Ablex.

Katz, L. and Chard, S. (1989) *Engaging Children's Minds: The Project Approach*, Ablex.

Katz, L. (2011) Conference 'Building a good Foundation', Huddersfield.

Miell, D., Phoenix, A., Thomas, K. (Eds) (2002) *Mapping Psychology 2*, Open University.

Moyles, J. (2007) *Early Years Foundations – Meeting the Challenge*, Open University Press.

Robson, S. (2006) *Developing thinking and understanding in Young Children*, Routledge.

Siraj-Blatchford, I. et al. (2002) Researching Effective Pedagogy in the Early Years (REPEY), DFES and the Institute of Education. Research Report 356.

Spaggiari, S. and Rinaldi, C. (1996) *The Hundred Languages of Children: Catalogue of the Exhibit*, Reggio Children Italy.

The Hundred Languages of Children, © 1996 Preschools and Infant-toddler Centers – Istituzione of the Municipality of Reggio Emilia, Italy, published by Reggio Children (www.reggiochildren.it).

Chapter 2

Bruce, T. (2004) *Cultivating Creativity in Babies, Toddlers and Young Children*, Hodder and Stoughton.

Claxton, G. (2009-June) Conference 'Thinking, Making and Learning: The foundations for a happy life'.

Craft, A. (2012) 'Child-initiated play and professional creativity: Enabling for year olds' possibility thinking', *Journal of Thinking skills and Creativity*, Vol 7 Issue 1.

Craft, A. (2010) Teaching for Possibility Thinking. What is it and how do we do it? *Learning Matters*, Vol 15, Number 1.

DCSF (2009) Learning, Playing and Interacting – Good practice in the EYFS.

Drummond, M.J (1993) *Assessing Children's Learning*, David Fulton Publishers.

Duffy, B. (1998) *Supporting Creativity and Imagination in the Early Years*, Open University Press.

References

Fumoto, H., Robson, S., Greenfield, S., Hargreaves, D. (2012) *Young Children's Creative Thinking*, Sage.

Giudici, C., Rinaldi, C. and Krechevsky, M. (2001) *Making learning visible: children as individual and group learners*, Reggio Children.

Laevers, F. (1994) in Pascal, C. and Bertram, T. *Effective Early Learning Programme, Child Involvement Scale*, University College Worcester.

Rich, D., Casanova, D., Dixon, A., Drummond, M.J, Durrant, A., Myer, C. (2005) *First hand experience – what matters to children*, Rich Learning Opportunities.

Siraj-Blatchford, I. et al. (2002) Researching Effective Pedagogy in the Early Years (REPEY), DFES and the Institute of Education. Research Report 356.

Chapter 3

Carr, M. (2001) *Assessment in Early Childhood Settings – Learning Stories*, Paul Chapman Publishing.

DCSF (2008) Early Years Foundation Stage (www.education.gov.uk).

DfE (2012) Statutory Framework for the Early Years Foundation Stage (www.education.gov.uk).

Giudici, C., Rinaldi, C. and Krechevsky, M. (2001) *Making learning visible: children as individual and group learners*, Reggio Children.

Gopnik, A., Meltzoff, A., Kuhl, P. (1999) *How Babies Think*, Phoenix.

Hawkins, C. and J. (1995) *Pat the Cat*, Dorling Kindersley Family Library.

Wright, S. (2010) *Understanding Creativity in Early Childhood*, Sage.

Chapter 4

DCSF (2008) Early Years Foundation Stage (www.education.gov.uk).

DCSF (2012) Finding and exploring young children's fascinations (www.education.gov.uk).

DfE (2012) Statutory Framework for the Early Years Foundation Stage (www.education.gov.uk).

Chilvers, D. (2012) Playing to learn – A guide to child-led play and its importance for thinking and learning (www.atl.org.uk).

Gussin-Paley, V. (2004) *A child's work the importance of fantasy play*, The University of Chicago Press.

Chapter 5

Isaacs, S. (1929) *The Nursery Years – The mind of the child from birth to six years*, Routledge.

Moore, M. (Ed) (2012) Cornerstones Curriculum (www.cornerstoneseducation.co.uk).

Moyles, J. et al. (2002) *Study of Pedagogical Effectiveness in Early Learning (SPEEL)*, DFES.

Siraj-Blatchford, I. et al. (2002) Researching Effective Pedagogy in the Early Years, DFES.

Sylva, K. et al. (2004) The Effective Provsion of Pre-School Education (EPPE) – The Final Report: Effective Pre-School Education, DFES and Institute of Education.

Acknowledgements

Writing this book has made me really think about how children learn and do their own thinking. It has been a real privilege to observe the children and listen to their stories and watch their ideas and interests as they became so involved. Children are truly wonderful creative thinkers.

My thanks to all the children who have shared their ideas, thoughts and words, especially to Jessica who has always been a creative thinker and to the babies, toddlers and children at Broomhall Nursery School and Children's Centre in Sheffield – a vibrant, exciting child-centred oasis with wonderful open-ended opportunities for children to think, explore and create. Also thanks to Tinsley Green Community Children's Centre in Sheffield – where there is a real community of children, parents and staff who work in partnership together creating a welcoming, stimulating child-led environment. I would like to thank the Reception Class at Carcroft Primary School in Doncaster – a school where being creative lies at the heart of the curriculum and children's ideas are celebrated. Thanks to Blake at Central Street School in Calderdale and Catherine Pidgeon, his creative teacher who sparked off the PLODs project and made us do a lot of thinking.

Thanks also go to Kath Priestley – Foundation Phase Lead at Carfield Primary School, Sheffield for sharing the Frosty Day observation and checking it all made sense, Ann Hinchcliffe – who knows where all the commas go and Emily Brunt for being my constant support.

Thanks go to the staff and parents of all the settings featured in the book for giving us permission to use the photos.

BRIDGWATER COLLEGE LRC